14
Kazuki Funatsu

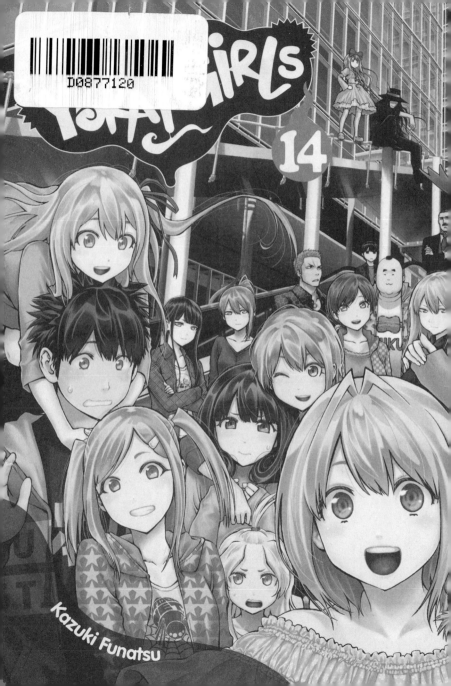

YŌKAI GIRLS

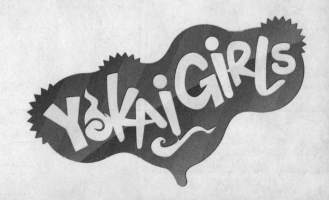

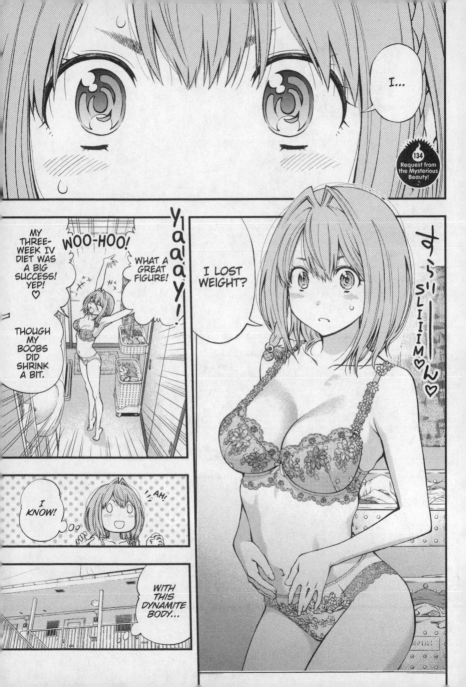

I...

YAAAY!

WOO-HOO!

MY THREE-WEEK IV DIET WAS A BIG SUCCESS! YEP! ♡

WHAT A GREAT FIGURE!

THOUGH MY BOOBS DID SHRINK A BIT.

I LOST WEIGHT?

SLIIIM ♡ ♡

I KNOW!

AH!

WITH THIS DYNAMITE BODY...

I'LL SEDUCE JUNKER-SAN!

POP

134
Request from the Mysterious Beauty! ♪

HNEERK

SNOOORE

EH HEH HEH HEH HEH! ♡

HE'S FAST ASLEEP!

JUNKER...

HOP

YEP, LET'S DO THIS!

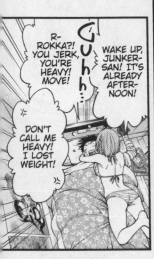

R-ROKKA?! YOU JERK, YOU'RE HEAVY! MOVE!

GUhh...

DON'T CALL ME HEAVY! I LOST WEIGHT!

WAKE UP, JUNKER-SAN! IT'S ALREADY AFTER-NOON!

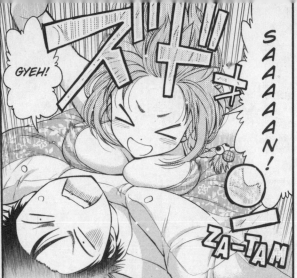

GYEH!

SAAAAN!

ZA-TAM

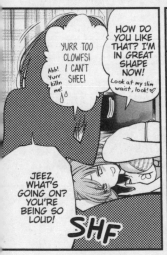

YURR TOO CLOWFSI

Ahh! I CAN'T YURR killn me! SHEEI

HOW DO YOU LIKE THAT? I'M IN GREAT SHAPE NOW! Look at my slim waist, look! ♡

JEEZ, WHAT'S GOING ON? YOU'RE BEING SO LOUD!

SHF

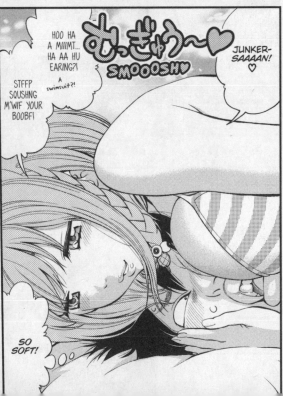

HOO HA A MIIIMT... HA AA HU EARING?! A swimsuit?!

STFFP SQUSHING M'WIF YOUR BOOBFI

むっぎゅう～♡ SMOOOSH♡

JUNKER-SAAAAN! ♡

SO SOFT!

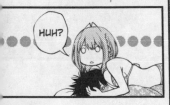

HUH?

Hnn!
THIS IS WAY TOO MUCH OF A RACKET THIS EARLY IN THE MORNING!
CAN'T WE HAVE A LITTLE MORE PEACE AND QUIET?
STRETCH
JIGGLE♡
Wahhhh!
H-H-H-H-HIME-CHAN?!
Huuuuh?!
HEY! WHAT'S GOING ON HERE, JUNKER-SAN?!
I-I DON'T KNOW! I HAVEN'T DONE ANYTHING!
HUH? YOU DON'T REMEMBER, HONEY?
THOSE FINGERS AND TONGUE PLAYED WITH EVERY SINGLE INCH OF MY BODY.
HE WENT WILD AND POUND-POUND-POUNDED ME FROM THE FRONT, FROM BEHIND, FOUR ROUNDS TOTAL!
A
AN!
A
AAN♡
AAN♡
IT WAS WONDERFUL! ♡
CLING♡
......

BA-THWACK
Wahhhhh!
YOU SLEAZE-BAG MAN-WHORE!
ばちこー
I DIDN'T DO ANY OF THAT!
DO I LOOK LIKE A GUY WHO HAS THE GUTS TO DO THAT?!
THAT'S RIGHT! IF YOU'RE GONNA LIE, COME UP WITH SOMETHING BETTER!
THAT CONVINCED YOU TOO FAST!
THEN I'LL MAKE IT TRUE RIGHT NOW!
ぐりんっ
SPIN
SOME PRIVACY, ROKKA? GET OUT!
WAMF...
SMOSH♡
I'M NOT LEAVING! NOPE!
GRAB
NO WAY AM I LETTING YOU DO THAT!
HYERP! ♡
SQUEEZE♡
WHAT?! YOU'RE TOO TIMID TO GO THAT FAR! DON'T GET IN OUR WAY!
I AM NOT!!
GYAA!
THEN STRIP!
GYAA!
GYAA!
HEY... WAIT, GUYS...
HERBF...
YEEK!!

HEY...
HEY! GIVE ME BACK MY BRA!
RUB
JIGGLE
RUB
JIGGLE
MURSH♡
NO WAY! IF YOU WANT IT BACK, THEN LET GO OF HIS THING!
NOM.
HOLD O--
CREAK
CREAK
OH, CRAP!
CREAK
CREAK
I... THINK I'M GONNA DIE...
CREAK
I'M CU...
CRACK
AH.
FOAM FOAM FOAM
Yeeeek!
JUNKER-SAN?!
HONEY? HONEY?!
NUUUU!

We have live aerial footage!!
Black smoke is billowing from this building in Marunouchi, Tokyo!
This is the home office of public-interest corporation GCUP.
The police have cordoned off the vicinity to maintain order.
What sort of company is GCUP?
We have little information on this organization yet, but...
A public-interest corporation is...
RIN...
YEAH.
YUKIMURA-SAN...
...
...
HUH?! WHAT'S THIS?
IS THIS GCUP?!
HUFF HUFF
BLEAH!
THE BUILDING'S ON FIRE!

WHAT IS THIS? WHAT'S GOING ON?!
MAYBE SOME YOKAI GOT SICK OF THEIR CRAP AND FOUGHT BACK?
I DON'T THINK SO. GCUP WOULDN'T LET THINGS GET THIS FAR.
DING DOOONG
!
IT'S CLEARLY SOME-THING SERIOUS, THOUGH.
I HOPE THIS MEANS THEY'RE DONE!
DING DONG
DING DONG
Aye, aye, so insistent.
AHH! WHO ARE YOU?!
HEY! YOU CAN'T JUST BARGE IN HERE!
OHH! THERE HE IS!
THE HEIR TO THE BLOOD OF SANJAKUBOU DAIGONGEN!
OHO, YOU'RE JUST AS ADORABLE AS I'VE HEARD!
HUH? WHO ARE YOU?!
HEY! YOU CAN'T JUST WALK INTO SOMEONE'S HOUSE!
HUH?
HUH?!

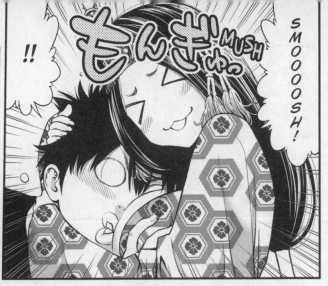

HUh?!

HEEEEY!

HOLD ON!

!!

MUSH

SMOOOOSH!

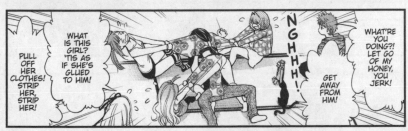

PULL OFF HER CLOTHES! STRIP HER, STRIP HER!

WHAT IS THIS GIRL? 'TIS AS IF SHE'S GLUED TO HIM!

NGHHH!

GET AWAY FROM HIM!

WHAT'RE YOU DOING?! LET GO OF MY HONEY, YOU JERK!

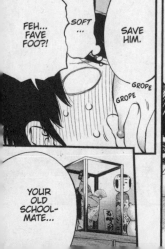

FEH... FAVE FOO?!

SOFT...

SAVE HIM.

GROPE

GROPE

YOUR OLD SCHOOL-MATE...

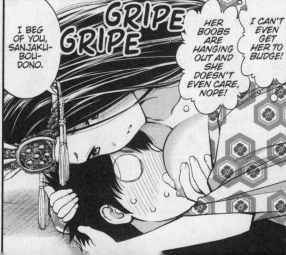

I BEG OF YOU, SANJAKU-BOU-DONO.

GRIPE GRIPE

HER BOOBS ARE HANGING OUT AND SHE DOESN'T EVEN CARE, NOPE!

I CAN'T EVEN GET HER TO BUDGE!

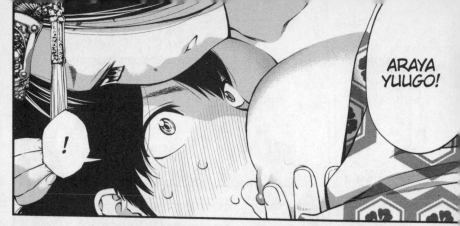

ARAYA
YUUGO!

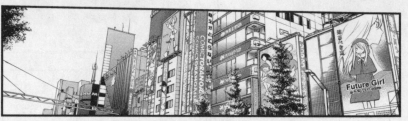

Just what
on Earth
is going on
inside that
building?!

News Flash
Reporting Live

BAM

Aah!
That
was the
sound
of yet
another
explosion!

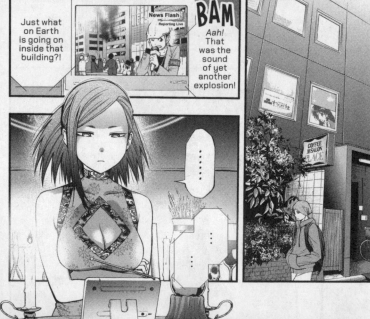

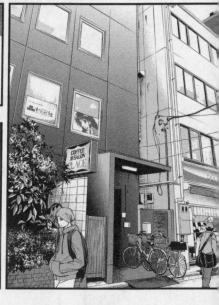

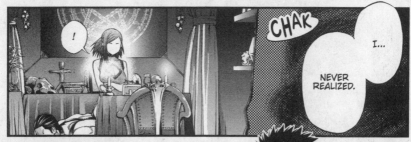

CHAK

I...

NEVER REALIZED.

THE NAME OF THIS SHOP...

BOY?

ZORRA-MAGICA.

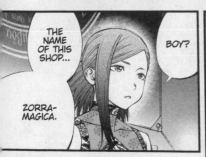

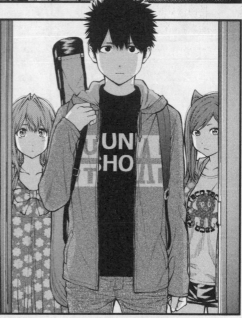

ZORRA IS SPANISH FOR FOX.

AND MAGICA LIKE... Y'KNOW, MAGIC.

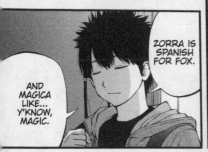

A YOUKO!

MAGIC FOX.

IN JAPANESE, THAT'S...

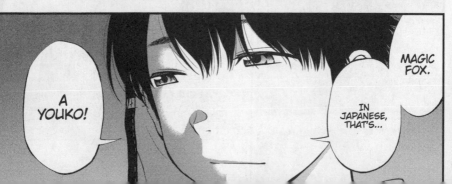

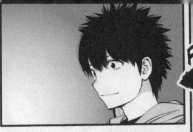

FWOO

IT WAS YOU, NAGI-SAN!

SO...

YOU'VE FINALLY FIGURED IT OUT.

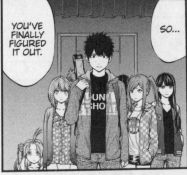

IN AN OLD PHOTO AT SHUU-YOU-JI TEMPLE...

THERE WAS SOMEONE WHO LOOKED JUST LIKE YOU. PLAINER, WITH SOFTER FEATURES, BUT THE RESEMBLANCE WAS THERE, NAGI-SAN.

NIA-CHAN WAS THE ONE WHO NOTICED THAT.

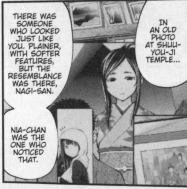

YOU'RE SUOU-BYAKUREN.

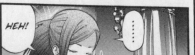

HEH!

......

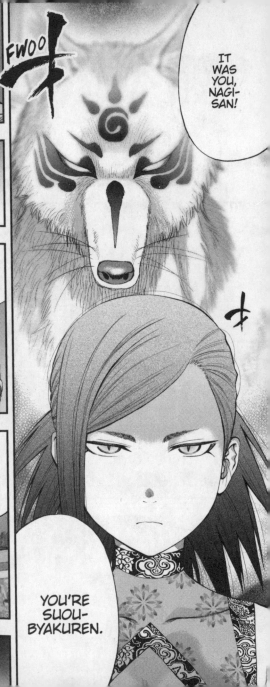

RUMBLE
SO YOU'RE SAYING I'M HARSH-FEATURED AND TOO FLASHY NOW?
RUMBLE
YEEEEP!!
NO! I DON'T MEAN THAT AT ALL!
PANIC
PANIC
You said too much, Junker-san.
ARE YOU...
GAKUJISHI?
EEEEEK!!
AS EXPECTED OF BYAKUREN-DONO! YOU CAN SEE THROUGH ME AT A GLANCE!
EXTRA-ORDINARY AS EVER!
IN-DEED.
SHWOOO
I AM THE ONE WHO IS FAMED FOR HER EXCEPTIONAL BEAUTY...
THE PEERLESS SHE-ONI...

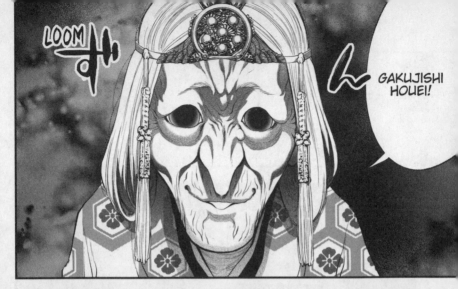

LOOM

GAKUJISHI HOUEI!

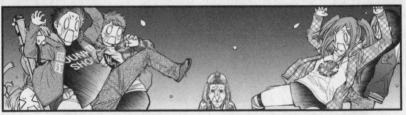

AND THE ONE RUNNING WILD AT GCUP HEAD-QUARTERS NOW IS...

YOU'RE THE ONE WHO GAVE ARAYA YUUGO THE POWER OF AN ONI AND HIGEKIRI, AREN'T YOU?!

SO YOU WERE INVOLVED, AFTER ALL!

WHAAAT?!

IT'S BEEN EVER SO LONG, BYAKU-REN-DONO! ♡

THOSE BOOBS... THOSE BOOBS?!

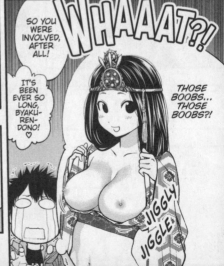

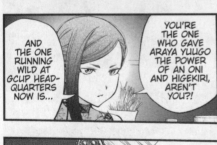

HE TOOK THE REST HIMSELF!

HEH HEH! I ONLY GAVE HIM THE VERY SLIGHTEST FRACTION OF AN ONI'S POWER.

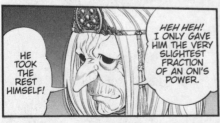

JIGGLY JIGGLE

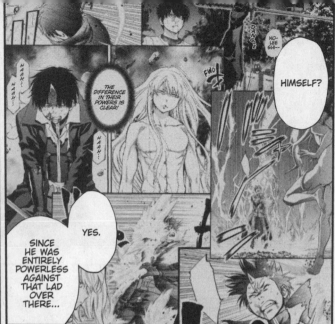

HE SOUGHT FURTHER POWER.

NAAH! NAAH!

THE DIFFERENCE IN THEIR POWERS IS CLEAR!

HO-LEE SH—

HIMSELF?

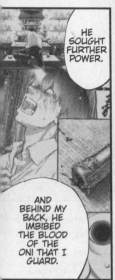

AND BEHIND MY BACK, HE IMBIBED THE BLOOD OF THE ONI THAT I GUARD.

NAAH!...

SINCE HE WAS ENTIRELY POWERLESS AGAINST THAT LAD OVER THERE...

YES.

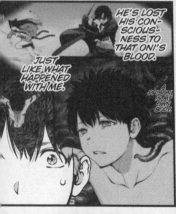

HE'S LOST HIS CON-SCIOUS-NESS TO THAT ONI'S BLOOD.

A PRISONER IN MY OWN BODY.

JUST LIKE WHAT HAPPENED WITH ME.

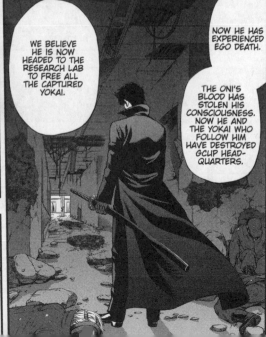

WE BELIEVE HE IS NOW HEADED TO THE RESEARCH LAB TO FREE ALL THE CAPTURED YOKAI.

NOW HE HAS EXPERIENCED EGO DEATH.

THE ONI'S BLOOD HAS STOLEN HIS CONSCIOUSNESS. NOW HE AND THE YOKAI WHO FOLLOW HIM HAVE DESTROYED GCUP HEAD-QUARTERS.

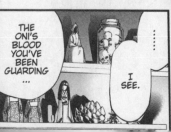

THE ONI'S BLOOD YOU'VE BEEN GUARDING...

......

I SEE.

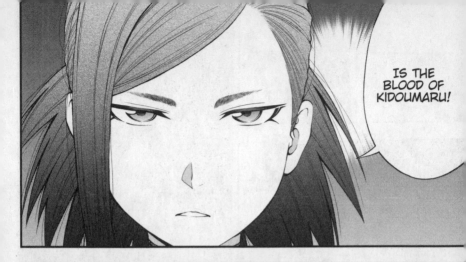

IS THE BLOOD OF KIDOUMARU!

Later, that woman gave birth to a child who was born with a full set of teeth. By the time it was seven or eight, they said it could kill boars and monkeys with the throw of a stone to eat them.

This child grew up to become Kidoumaru, and he left the capitol to hunt Yorimitsu's parents in revenge for Shuten Douji.

KIDOUMARU

The "dou" part of this yokai's name can be written with the character for "child" or the character for "same." One of the three most evil yokai in Japan, Kidoumaru is said to be the child of Shuten Douji.

When Minamoto Yorimitsu defeated Shuten Douji, the women the fiend had captured were returned to their homes. Alas, one of them had since gone mad.

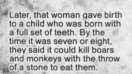

......

PLEASE... PUT A STOP TO HIS MADNESS!

THE POWER OF THE ONI HAS GROWN BEYOND HIS CONTROL.

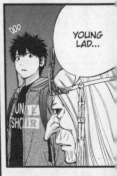

YOUNG LAD...

OF COURSE I'LL STOP HIM.
HE'S MY FRIEND!
NAGI-SAN...
AS YOU COMMAND.

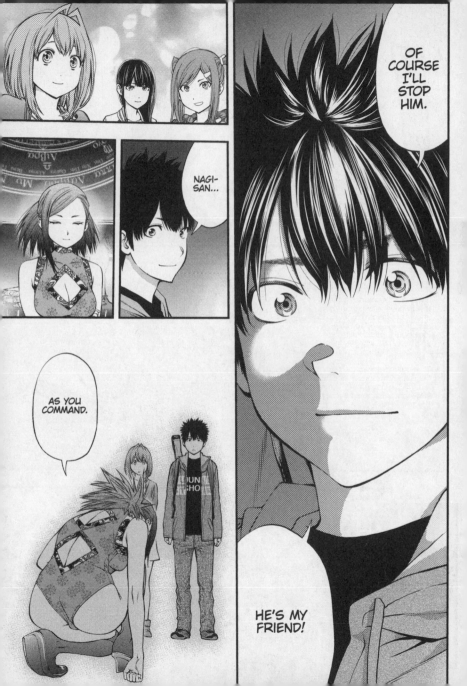

LET'S GO!
BAM
Party at Pasela!
PASELA RESORTS GROUP
Luxury Capsule Hotel
Anshin Oyado
300 OK!

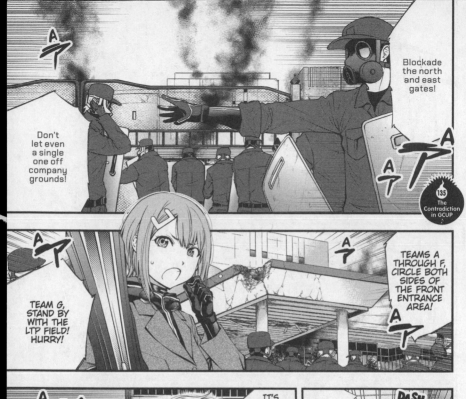

Blockade the north and east gates!

Don't let even a single one off company grounds!

TEAMS A THROUGH F, CIRCLE BOTH SIDES OF THE FRONT ENTRANCE AREA!

TEAM G, STAND BY WITH THE LTP FIELD! HURRY!

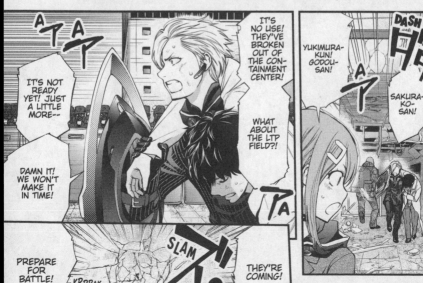

IT'S NO USE! THEY'VE BROKEN OUT OF THE CONTAINMENT CENTER!

WHAT ABOUT THE LTP FIELD?!

IT'S NOT READY YET! JUST A LITTLE MORE--

DAMN IT! WE WON'T MAKE IT IN TIME!

PREPARE FOR BATTLE!

KRRRAK

SLAM

THEY'RE COMING!

YUKIMURA-KUN! GODOU-SAN!

SAKURAKO-SAN!

DASH

KRAKA
KOOOOOSH
WHOOSH
135
The Contradiction in GCUP ♪

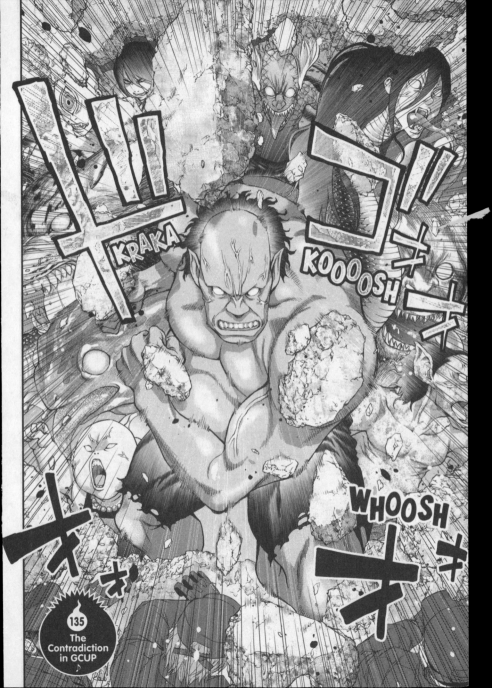

Wahh!
They've broken through the wall?!
Shit!
A
Gyah!
A
TSK!
ZWING
BLAM
BLAM
A
Gyah!
BAM
BSHHT
FWOOOSH
Grrgh ...
HYA!
SWEEP
HOP
YA

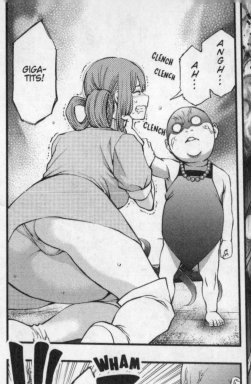

GIGA-TITS!

CLENCH
CLENCH

CLENCH

AH...

ANGH!...

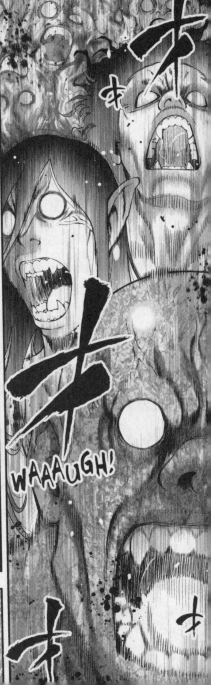

WAAAUGH!

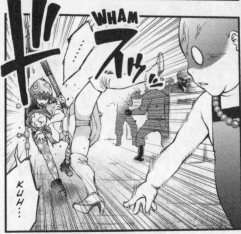

WHAM

ド!

スト!

KUH...

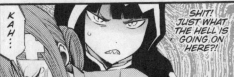

KAH...

SHIT!
JUST WHAT
THE HELL IS
GOING ON
HERE?!

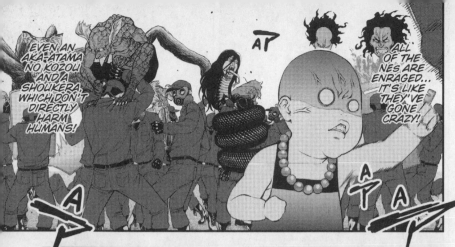

EVEN AN AKA-ATAMA NO KOZOU AND A SHOUKERA, WHICH DON'T DIRECTLY HARM HUMANS!

ALL OF THE NES ARE ENRAGED... IT'S LIKE THEY'VE GONE CRAZY!

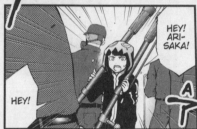

HEY! ARI-SAKA!

HEY!

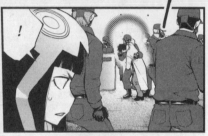

!

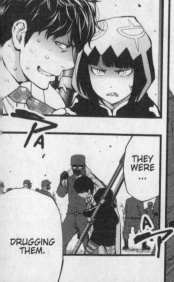

WHY THE HELL ARE THEY SO PISSED OFF?!

THEY WERE...

DRUGGING THEM.

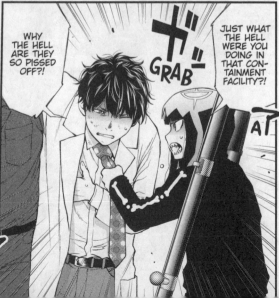

GRAB

JUST WHAT THE HELL WERE YOU DOING IN THAT CONTAINMENT FACILITY?!

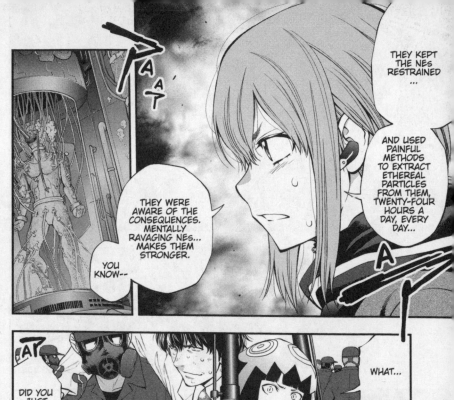

THEY KEPT THE NEs RESTRAINED...

AND USED PAINFUL METHODS TO EXTRACT ETHEREAL PARTICLES FROM THEM, TWENTY-FOUR HOURS A DAY, EVERY DAY...

THEY WERE AWARE OF THE CONSEQUENCES. MENTALLY RAVAGING NEs... MAKES THEM STRONGER.

YOU KNOW--

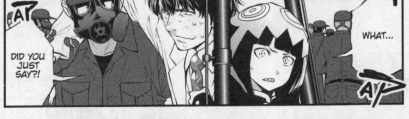

WHAT...

DID YOU JUST SAY?!

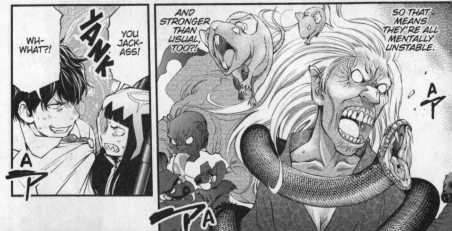

WH-WHAT?!

YOU JACK-ASS!

AND STRONGER THAN USUAL, TOO?!

SO THAT MEANS THEY'RE ALL MENTALLY UNSTABLE.

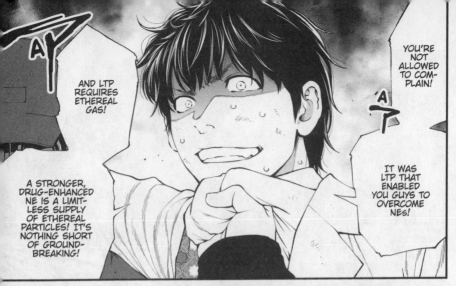

AND LTP REQUIRES ETHEREAL GAS!

YOU'RE NOT ALLOWED TO COMPLAIN!

A STRONGER, DRUG-ENHANCED NE IS A LIMITLESS SUPPLY OF ETHEREAL PARTICLES! IT'S NOTHING SHORT OF GROUNDBREAKING!

IT WAS LTP THAT ENABLED YOU GUYS TO OVERCOME NEs!

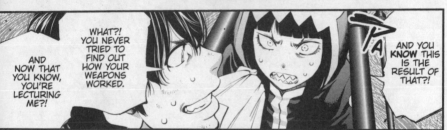

AND NOW THAT YOU KNOW, YOU'RE LECTURING ME?!

WHAT?! YOU NEVER TRIED TO FIND OUT HOW YOUR WEAPONS WORKED.

AND YOU KNOW THIS IS THE RESULT OF THAT?!

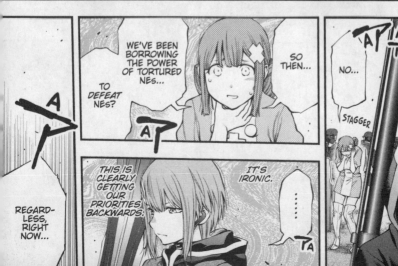

WE'VE BEEN BORROWING THE POWER OF TORTURED NEs...

TO DEFEAT NEs?

SO THEN...

NO...

STAGGER

REGARDLESS, RIGHT NOW...

THIS IS CLEARLY GETTING OUR PRIORITIES BACKWARDS.

IT'S IRONIC.

......

WE MUST FIGHT!
BLAM
BLAM
SHWING
FOR THOSE WHOSE LIVES ENDED SUDDENLY, WITHOUT REASON...
AND FOR THOSE WHO SUFFERED THE LOSS OF THEIR STOLEN LOVED ONES.
NO MATTER THE METHODS, IF THERE'S A WAY WE CAN FIGHT...

A
A
THEN WE WILL!
A
A
YUKI-MURA-SAN...
A
GORILLA ...
A
A
TA
A

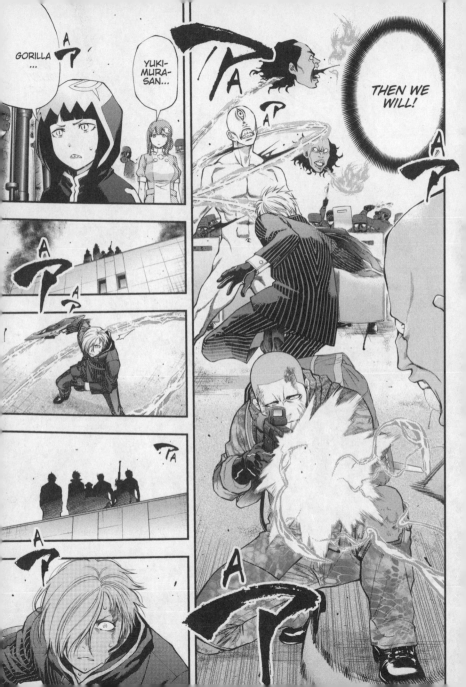

AH...

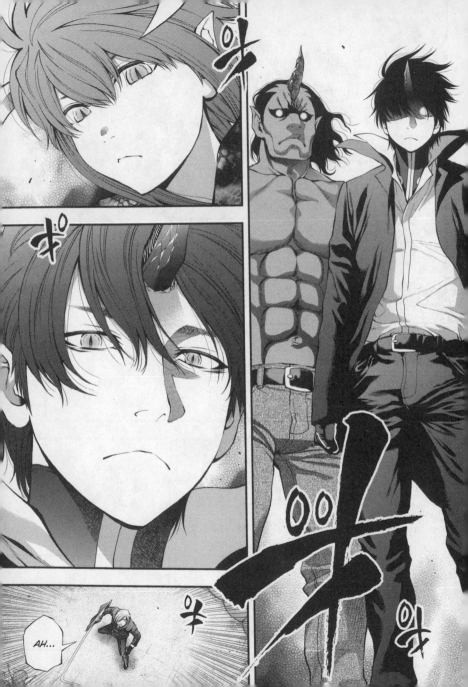

ARAAAAAAAAH!
A
A
A
A

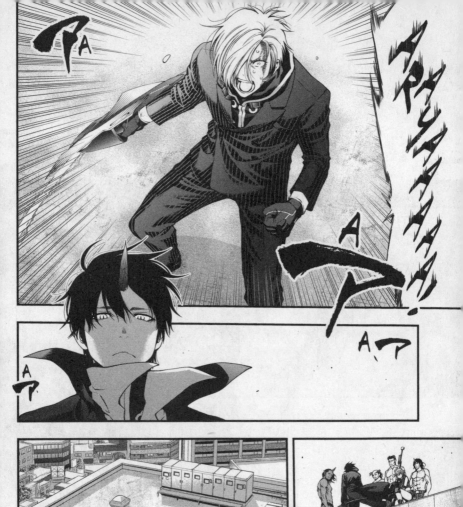

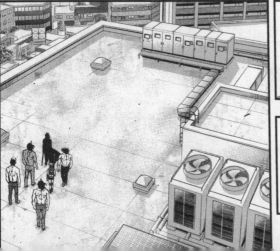

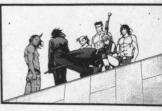

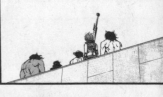

WE WILL GAIN CONTROL OF THIS CITY.
GO, MY HELLISH ARMY!
GRRR
GRRRRR
WOOSH

ZBABABAAAM

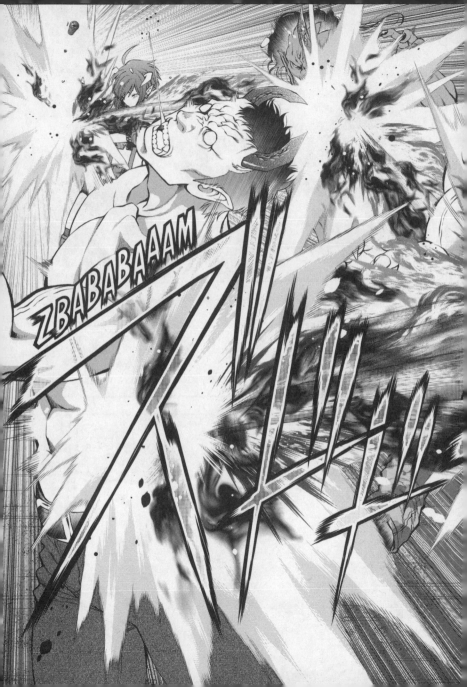

GUH...
GAH...

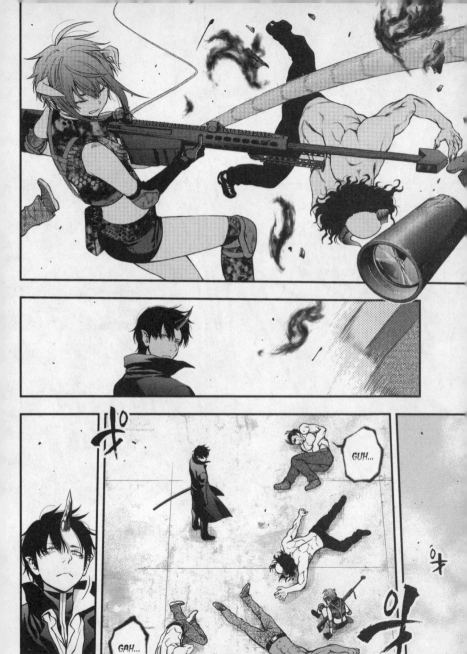

I'M GONNA STOP YOU, YUUGO!
BAM

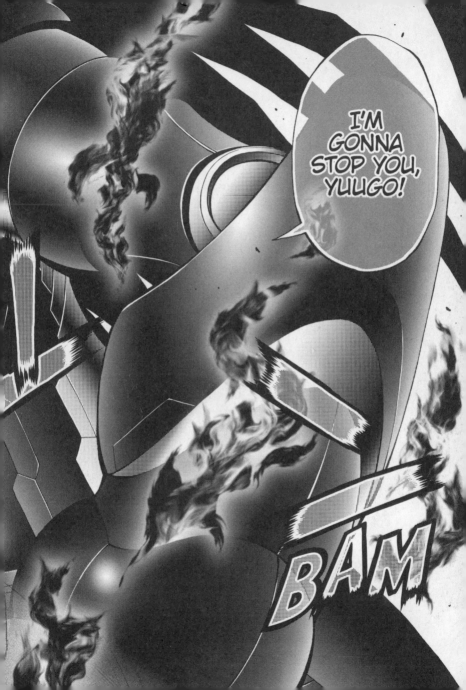

THIS TIME, IT'S MY TURN!

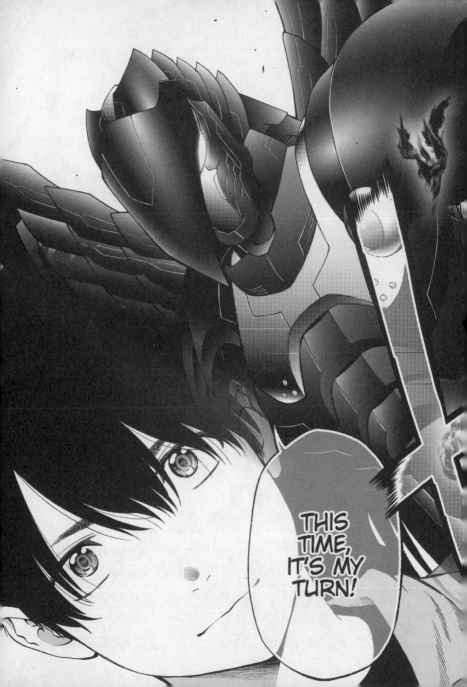

Extra: That's crazy...

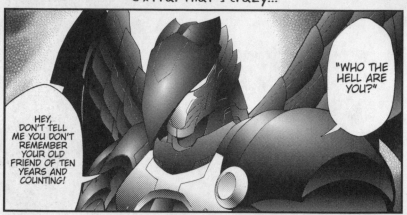

"WHO THE HELL ARE YOU?"

HEY, DON'T TELL ME YOU DON'T REMEMBER YOUR OLD FRIEND OF TEN YEARS AND COUNTING!

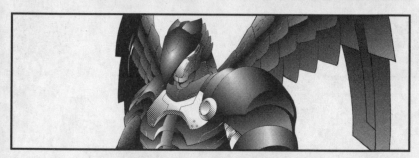

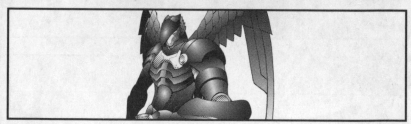

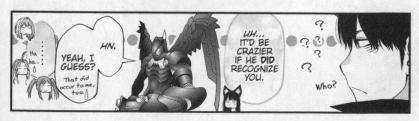

Ha ha......

YEAH, I GUESS?

HN.

That did occur to me, too.

UH... IT'D BE CRAZIER IF HE DID RECOGNIZE YOU.

? ? ? ? ?

Who?

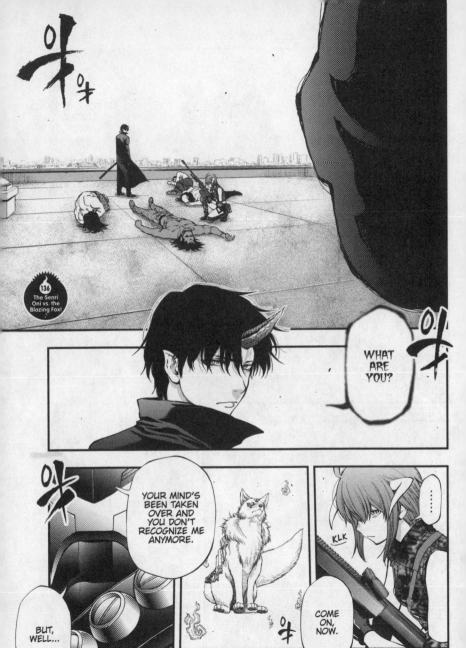

136
The Senri
Oni vs. the
Blazing Fox!

WHAT
ARE
YOU?

YOUR MIND'S
BEEN TAKEN
OVER AND
YOU DON'T
RECOGNIZE ME
ANYMORE.

KLK

・・・・・

BUT,
WELL...

COME
ON,
NOW.

136
The Senri Oni vs. the Blazing Fox! ♪
GUESS THAT'S NO SURPRISE.
There's no Yatsuki identifiers here.
BAM

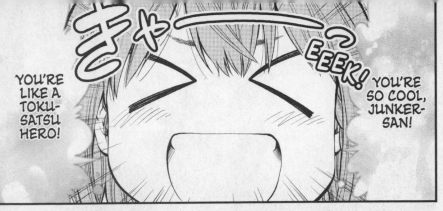

YOU'RE LIKE A TOKU- SATSU HERO!

EEEK!

YOU'RE SO COOL, JUNKER- SAN!

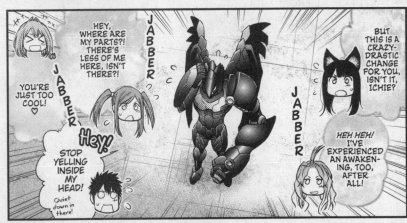

HEY, WHERE ARE MY PARTS?! THERE'S LESS OF ME HERE, ISN'T THERE?!

JABBER

YOU'RE JUST TOO COOL! ♡

JABBER

Hey!

STOP YELLING INSIDE MY HEAD!

Quiet down in there!

JABBER

BUT THIS IS A CRAZY- DRASTIC CHANGE FOR YOU, ISN'T IT, ICHIE?

HEH HEH! I'VE EXPERIENCED AN AWAKEN- ING, TOO, AFTER ALL!

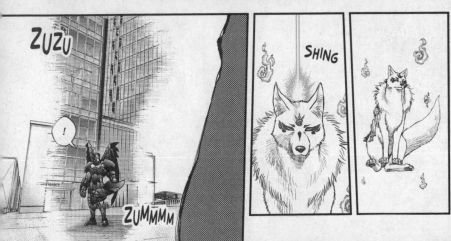

ZUZU

!

ZUMMMM

SHING

와
Smile!
와

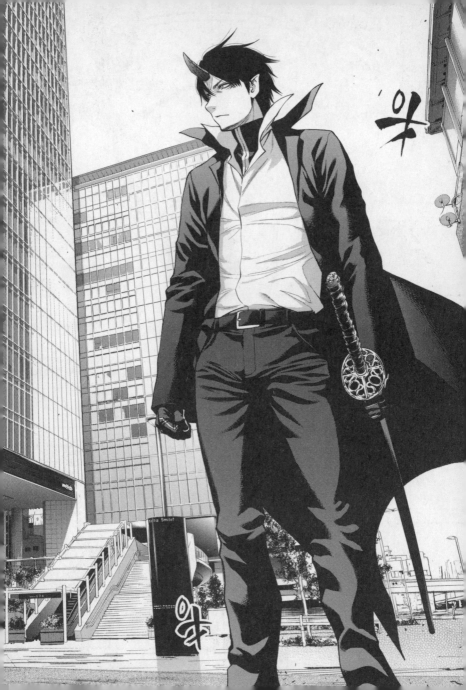

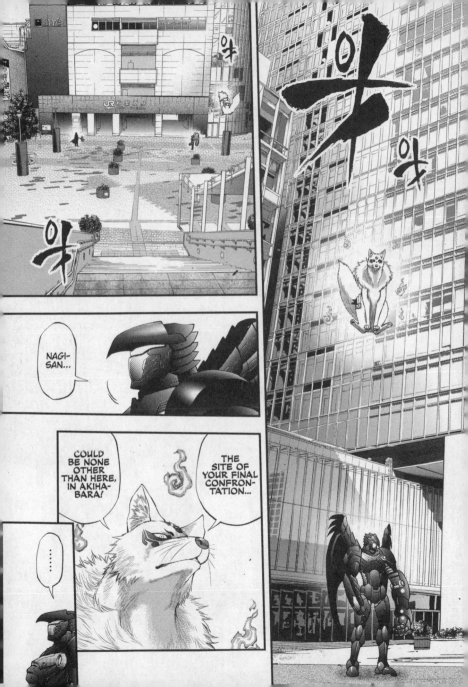

NAGI-
SAN...

COULD
BE NONE
OTHER
THAN HERE,
IN AKIHA-
BARA!

THE
SITE OF
YOUR FINAL
CONFRON-
TATION...

......

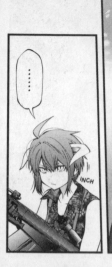

......

INCH

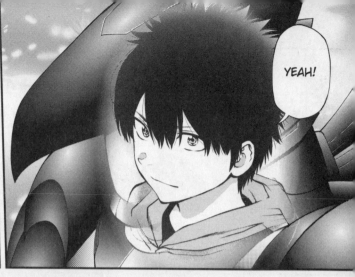

YEAH!

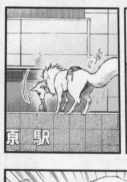

京駅

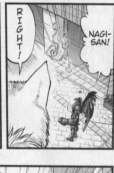

RIGHT!

NAGI-SAN!

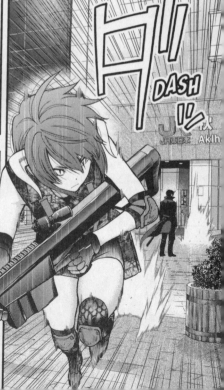

ブ DASH

JR AkIh

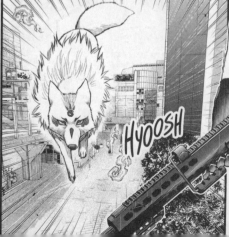

HYOOSH

Tax Free
SHE'S FASTER THAN I THOUGHT.
WHERE DID SHE GO?
BTAM
BKSHT
YIP!

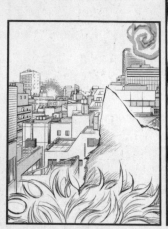

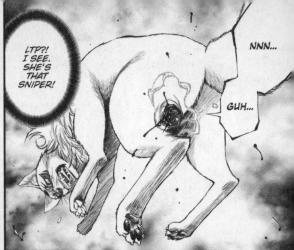

LTP?! I SEE. SHE'S THAT SNIPER!

NNN...

GUH...

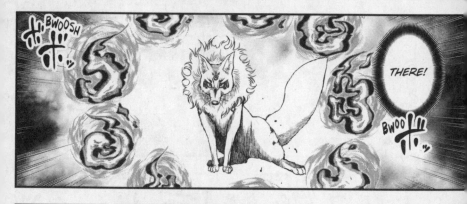

BWOOSH

THERE!

BWOO

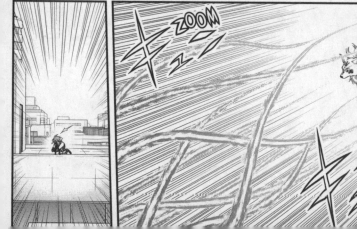

ZOOM

KSHOOM

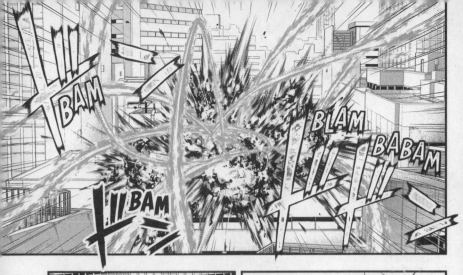

WOOOSH

DID I GET HER?

I'M PRETTY SURE I AT LEAST DAMAGED HER SCOPE.

TO HIT FROM THAT DISTANCE WITH NO SIGHT...

HER EYES, EH?

SHE'S AN ONI WITH VISUAL ABILI- TIES.

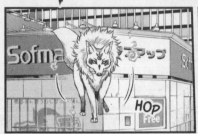

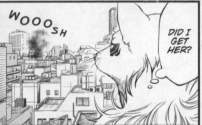

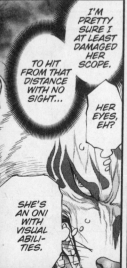

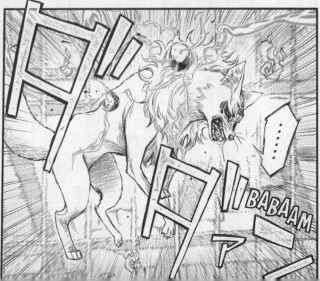

BABAAM

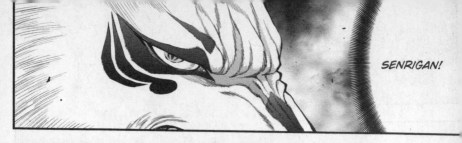

SENRIGAN!

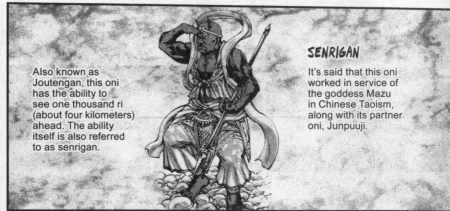

SENRIGAN

It's said that this oni worked in service of the goddess Mazu in Chinese Taoism, along with its partner oni, Junpuuji.

Also known as Joutengan, this oni has the ability to see one thousand ri (about four kilometers) ahead. The ability itself is also referred to as senrigan.

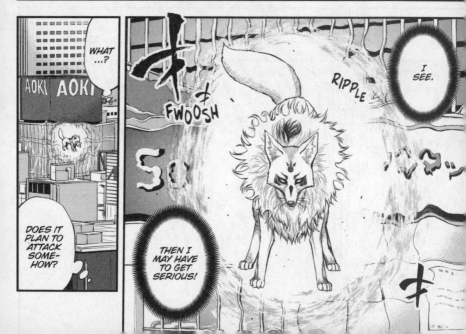

WHAT ...?

DOES IT PLAN TO ATTACK SOME- HOW?

FWOOSH

RIPPLE

I SEE.

THEN I MAY HAVE TO GET SERIOUS!

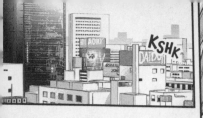

KSHK

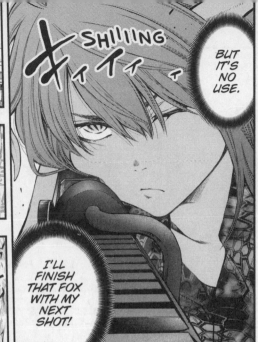

SHIIING

BUT IT'S NO USE.

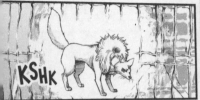

KSHK

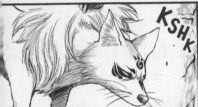

KSHK

I'LL FINISH THAT FOX WITH MY NEXT SHOT!

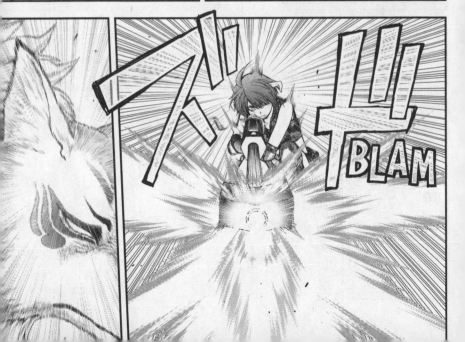

BLAM

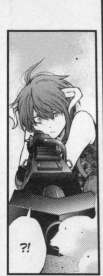

?!

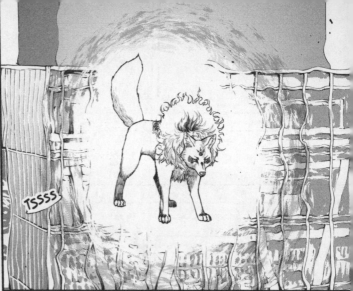

TSSSS

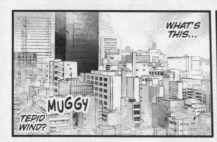

WHAT'S THIS...

MUGGY

TEPID WIND?

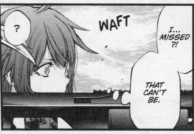

?

WAFT

I... MISSED ?!

THAT CAN'T BE.

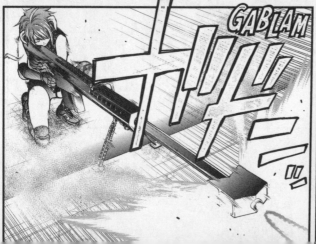

GABLAM

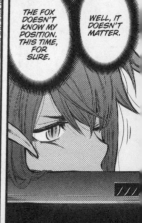

THE FOX DOESN'T KNOW MY POSITION. THIS TIME, FOR SURE.

WELL, IT DOESN'T MATTER.

TSSS

POP

FWAA

EVEN THE TUNGSTEN USED IN THE CORE OF THAT ARMOR-PIERCING AMMUNITION MELTS AT 5,555 DEGREES!

AND COPPER IS 2,571.

THE BOILING POINT OF LEAD IS 1,750 DEGREES.

WHA...?!

IN MY SCORCHING-HOT, TEN-THOUSAND-DEGREE SPACE...
IT'S IMPOSSIBLE FOR YOUR BULLETS TO EVEN EXIST!
KA
MA
WHAT ...
DID IT SAY?
I'VE FOUND YOU!

BLAM
YOU ...
BA-BLAM
BAM
BLAM
MON-
STER!
FWOOO
TSS
TSSS
AHH!!

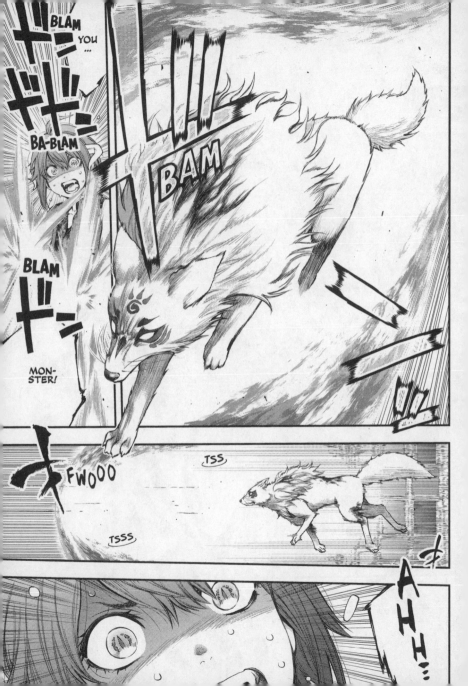

燼滅焔狐!!!!
BLAZING FOX OF INCINERATION!

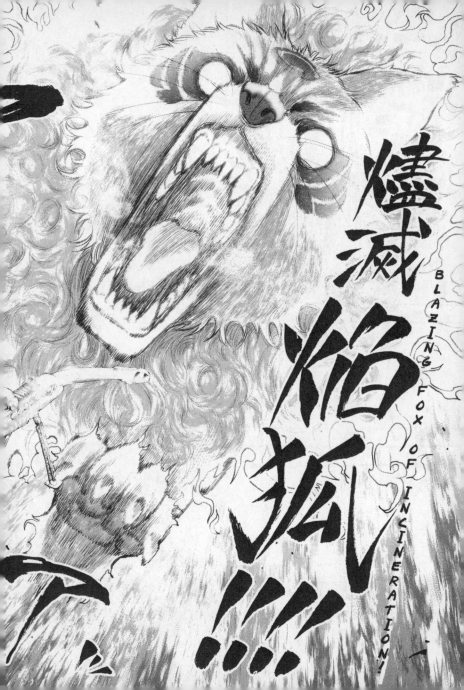

FWAA
AH...
......
BWOOSH
FWOO
TUP

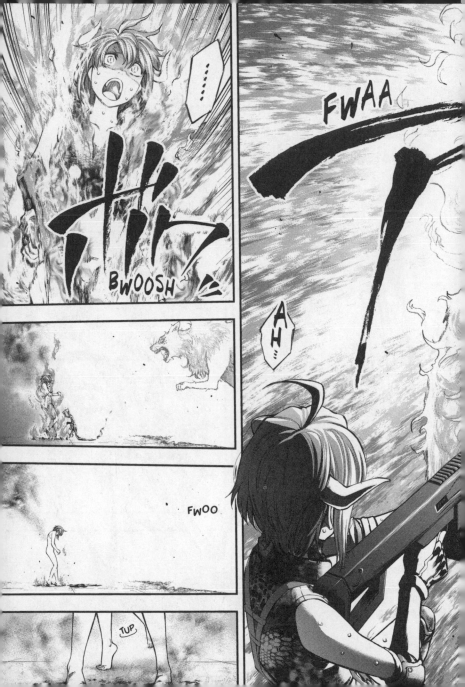

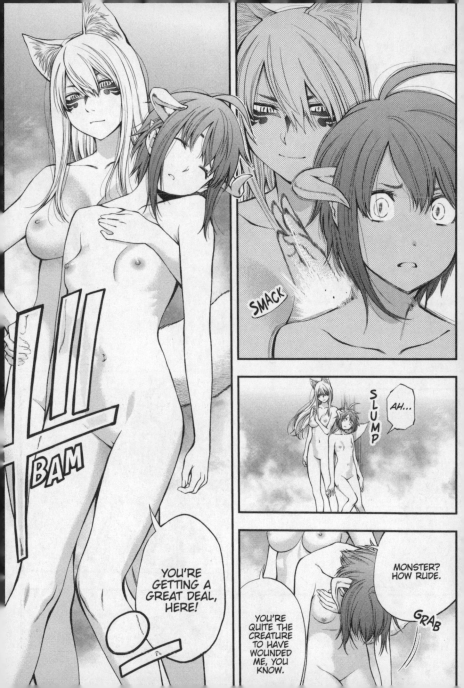

SMACK

BAM

SLUMP

AH...

YOU'RE
GETTING A
GREAT DEAL,
HERE!

MONSTER?
HOW RUDE.

YOU'RE
QUITE THE
CREATURE
TO HAVE
WOUNDED
ME, YOU
KNOW.

GRAB

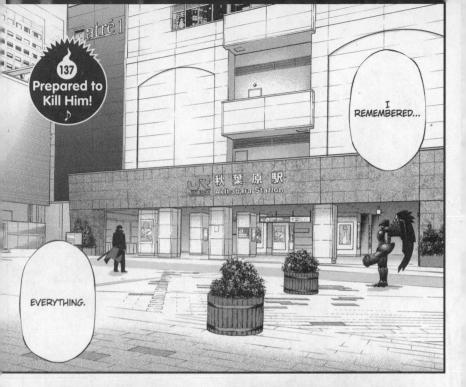

I REMEMBERED...

EVERYTHING.

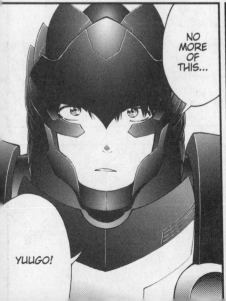

NO MORE OF THIS...

YUUGO!

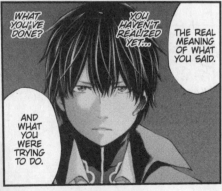

WHAT YOU'VE DONE?

YOU HAVEN'T REALIZED YET...

THE REAL MEANING OF WHAT YOU SAID.

AND WHAT YOU WERE TRYING TO DO.

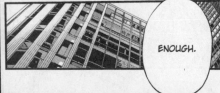

ENOUGH.

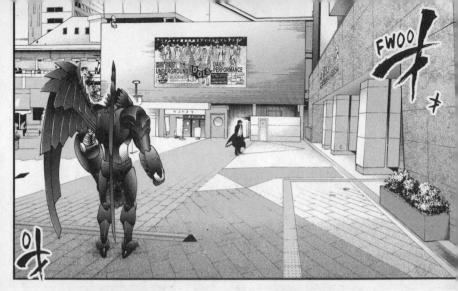

FWOO

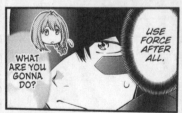

HE PROBABLY DOESN'T EVEN KNOW WHO I AM.

HE'S NOT LISTEN-ING TO ME.

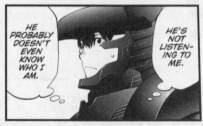

WHAT ARE YOU GONNA DO?

USE FORCE AFTER ALL.

EVEN IF HE DOES KNOW, HE WON'T BE ABLE TO DO ANYTHING.

OR, IF HE'S LIKE HOW I WAS THEN...

I WAS AWARE

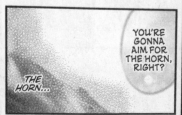

THE HORN...

YOU'RE GONNA AIM FOR THE HORN, RIGHT?

THAT MEANS I HAVE TO...

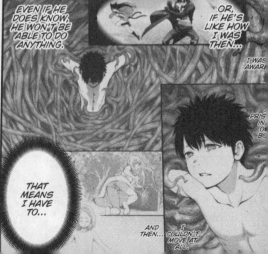

PRIS IN O BO

AND THEN... COULDN'T MOVE AT ALL.

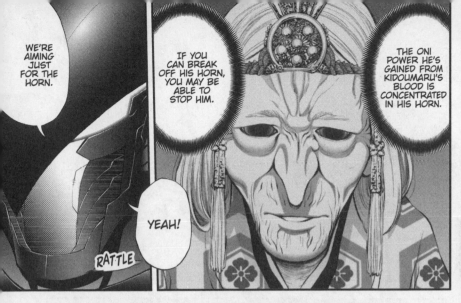

WE'RE AIMING JUST FOR THE HORN.

IF YOU CAN BREAK OFF HIS HORN, YOU MAY BE ABLE TO STOP HIM.

THE ONI POWER HE'S GAINED FROM KIDOUMARU'S BLOOD IS CONCENTRATED IN HIS HORN.

YEAH!

RATTLE

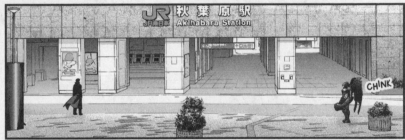

JR 秋葉原駅
Akihabara Station

CHINK

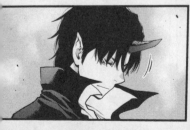

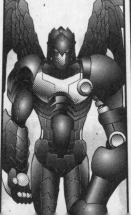

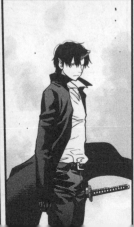

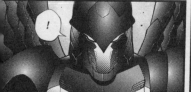

!

!!
SKRING
!
ROKKA!
PAANYAA
NYAAAAN!
BAM
HE'S FAST!
ICCHAN!
HOW DO YOU LIKE THAT?! I EN-DURED IT!
!!

WOOSH
LEAN
ZOOM
ZOOM
!
ZOOM
WAK
......
GWIIING
KUH...
WIFF

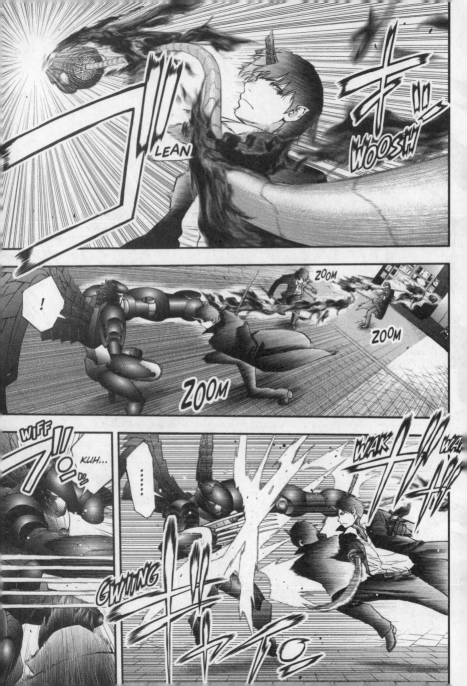

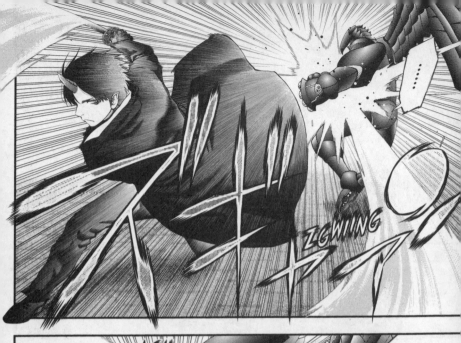

ZGWIING

YATSUKI! HIS STRIKES ARE POTENT! I CAN'T WITHSTAND THEM INDEFINITELY!

DASH DASH

DAMN IT!

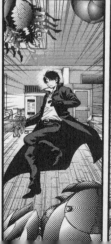

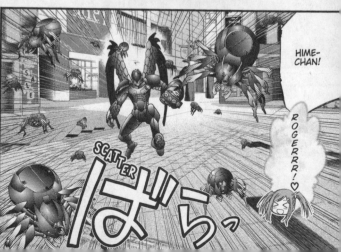

HIME-CHAN!

SCATTER

ROGERRR! ♥

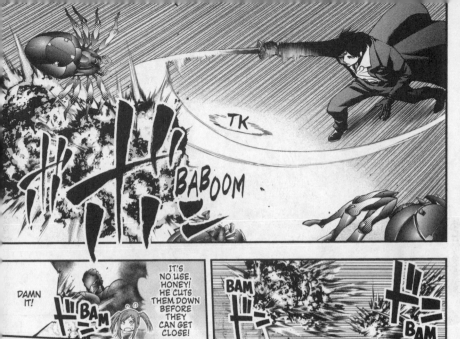

TK

BABOOM

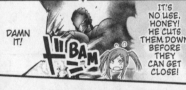

DAMN IT!

BAM

IT'S NO USE, HONEY! HE CUTS THEM DOWN BEFORE THEY CAN GET CLOSE!

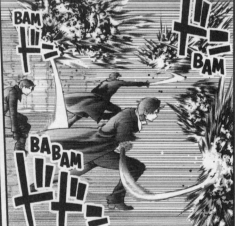

BAM

BAM

BABAM

!!

WOOSH

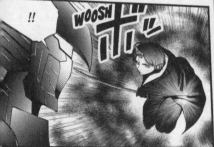

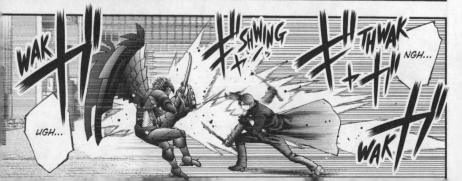

WAK

SHWING

THWAK

NGH...

UGH...

WAK

HRYAH!
WIFF!!
GAH...
CLANG
KUH...
NGH ...
YOU CAN'T JUST AIM FOR THE HORN, JUNKER!
VARY YOUR AT- TACKS!
DAMN IT! ROKKA!
PANYAAAA!!
BAM
WOOSH

ZOOM
!
ZAZOOM
HOP
SWOOSH
HIME-CHAN!
PSHHT
SWIPE
SWIPE
!!

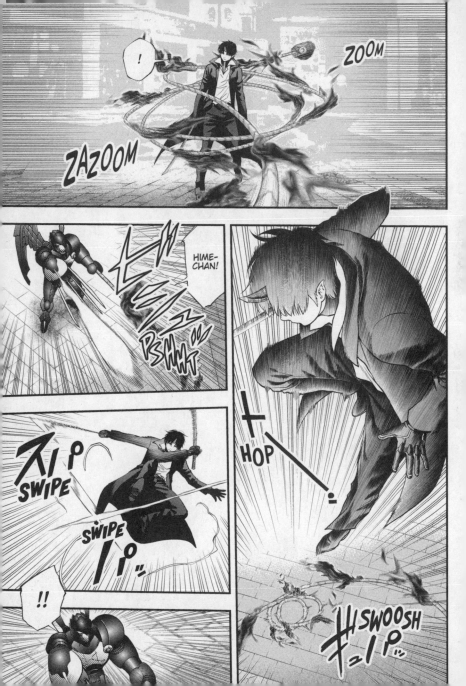

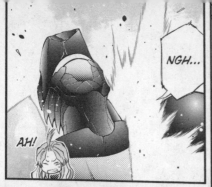

NGH...

AH!

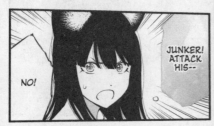

NO!

JUNKER! ATTACK HIS--

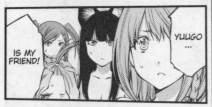

IS MY FRIEND!

YUUGO...

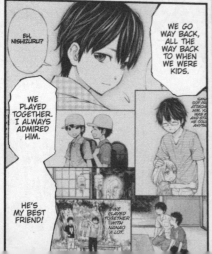

EH, NISHIZURU?

WE GO WAY BACK, ALL THE WAY BACK TO WHEN WE WERE KIDS.

WE PLAYED TOGETHER. I ALWAYS ADMIRED HIM.

NANA GOT ATTACKED. HIM. YUUGO WAS AND STOP HE COUL ANYTH

HE'S MY BEST FRIEND!

WE PLAYED TOGETHER WITH NANAO A LOT.

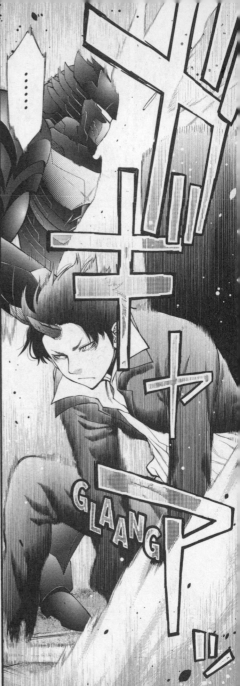

GLAANG

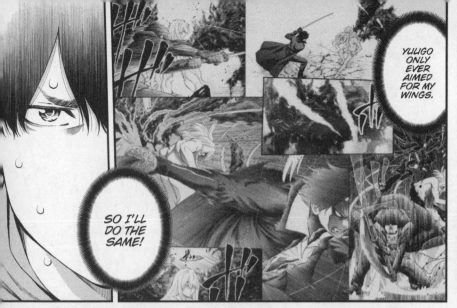

YUUGO ONLY EVER AIMED FOR MY WINGS.

SO I'LL DO THE SAME!

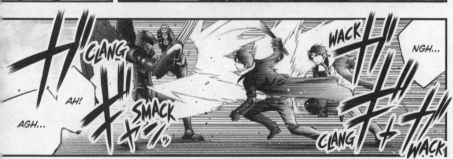

H'!
CLANG
H'!
SMACK
AH!
AGH...

WACK
H'!
NGH...
CLANG
WACK

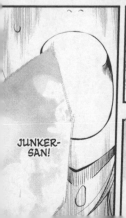

JUNKER-SAN!

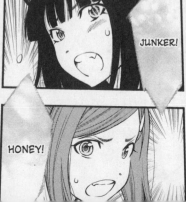

JUNKER!

HONEY!

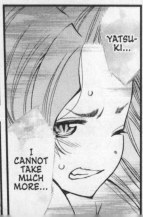

YATSU-KI...

I CANNOT TAKE MUCH MORE...

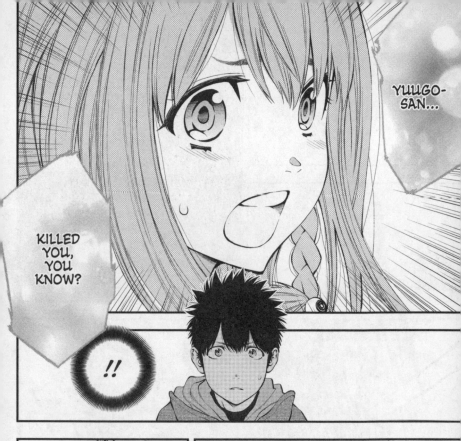

YUUGO-SAN...

KILLED YOU, YOU KNOW?

!!

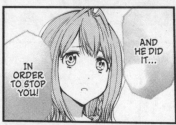

IN ORDER TO STOP YOU!

AND HE DID IT...

I'M SURE HE DIDN'T WANT TO DO IT...

BUT EVEN IF IT WAS TO STOP YOU...

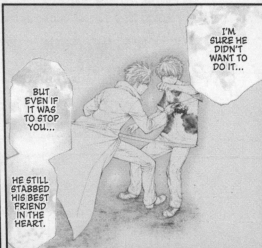

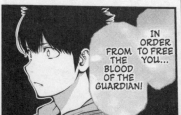

IN ORDER TO FREE YOU...

FROM THE BLOOD OF THE GUARDIAN!

HE STILL STABBED HIS BEST FRIEND IN THE HEART.

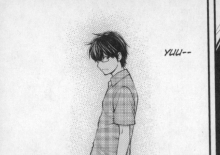

YUUI--

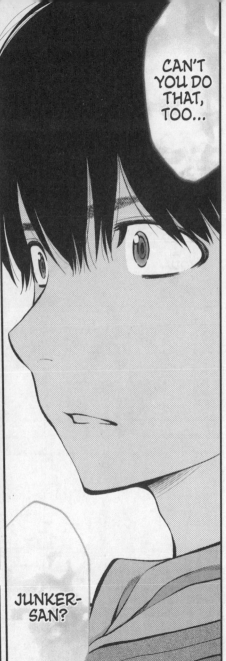

CAN'T YOU DO THAT, TOO...

JUNKER-SAN?

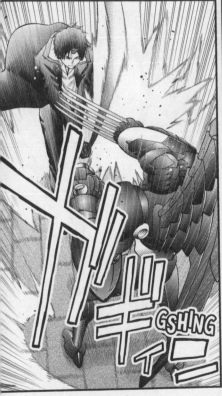

GSHING

OH...

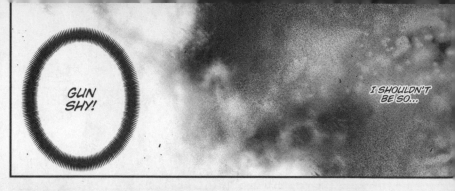

GUN SHY!

I SHOULDN'T BE SO...

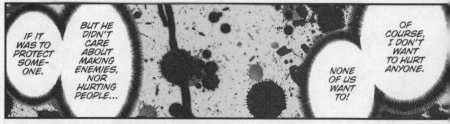

IF IT WAS TO PROTECT SOMEONE.

BUT HE DIDN'T CARE ABOUT MAKING ENEMIES, NOR HURTING PEOPLE...

NONE OF US WANT TO!

OF COURSE, I DON'T WANT TO HURT ANYONE.

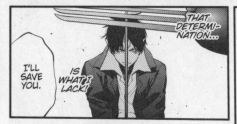

THAT DETERMINATION...

I'LL SAVE YOU.

IS WHAT I LACK!!

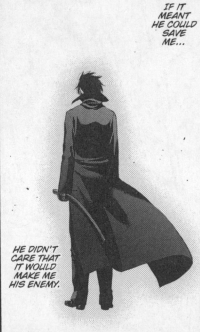

IF IT MEANT HE COULD SAVE ME...

HE DIDN'T CARE THAT IT WOULD MAKE ME HIS ENEMY.

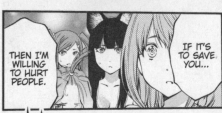

THEN I'M WILLING TO HURT PEOPLE.

IF IT'S TO SAVE YOU...

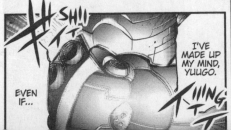

SHII T

I'VE MADE UP MY MIND, YUUGO.

KIING T

EVEN IF...

I HAVE TO KILL YOU TO DO IT...
I'M GOING TO SAVE YOU!
......
SLAM

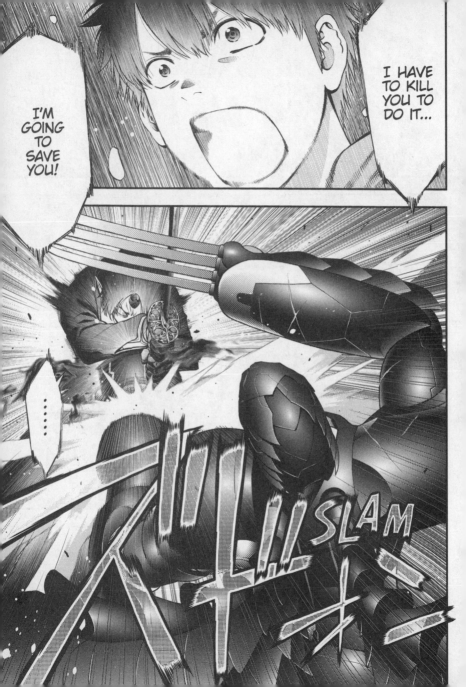

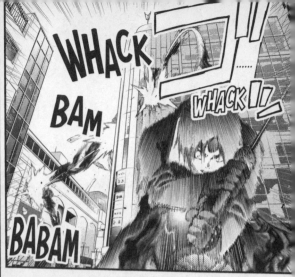

WHACK

BAM

WHACK

BABAM

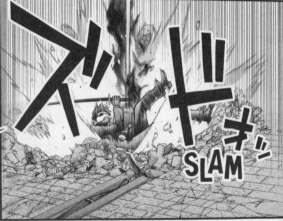

連撃頭突き!!!!

RAPID-FIRE HEADBUTT!

SLAM

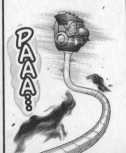

PAAAA...

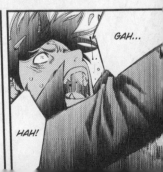

GAH...

HAH!

KABAM
NYA NYA NYA NYA NYA NYA NYA—!…
BAM
BAM
BAM
BAM
BAM
BAM

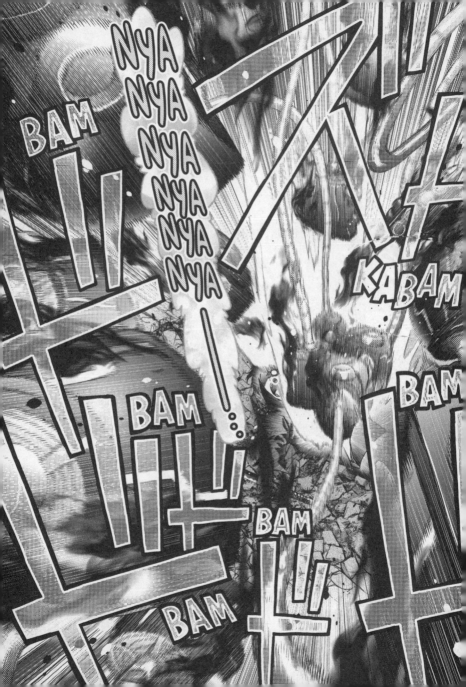

RATTLE
CRUMBLE
CRUMBLE

KCHINK

YUUGO...
HOTTEST UNDERGROUND IDOLS DAILY PERFORMANCE
WAKE UP!

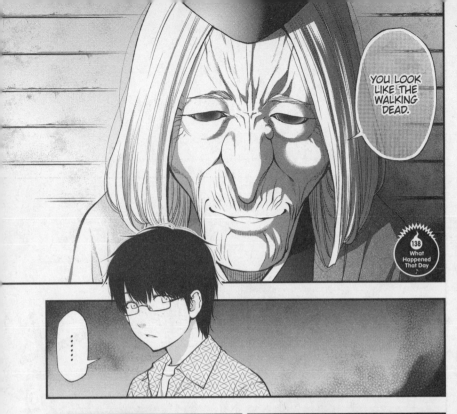

YOU LOOK LIKE THE WALKING DEAD.

138
What Happened That Day

. . . . . .

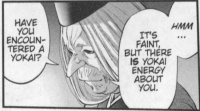

HAVE YOU ENCOUNTERED A YOKAI?

HMM...

IT'S FAINT, BUT THERE IS YOKAI ENERGY ABOUT YOU.

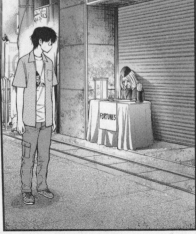

FORTUNES

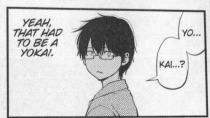

YEAH, THAT HAD TO BE A YOKAI.

YO...

KAI...?

138
What Happened That Day ♪
IT WAS A TENGU.

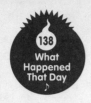

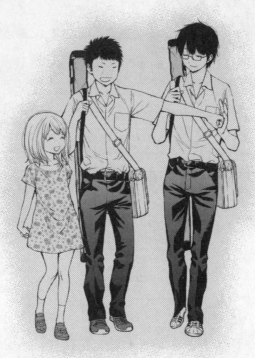

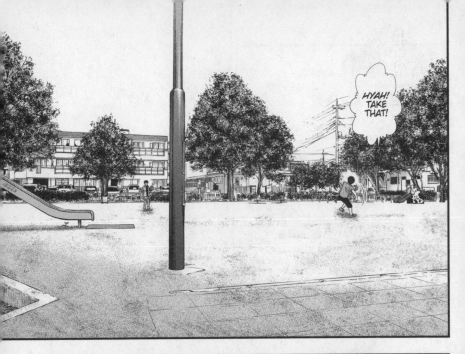

HYAH! TAKE THAT!

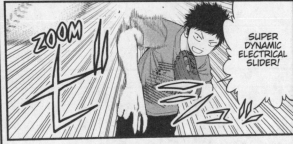

NO! IT WAS JUST SLIIIIGHTLY WOBBLY!

MAKE IT BEND, NOT WOBBLE.

If it's a slider, lol.

SUPER DYNAMIC ELECTRICAL SLIDER!

ZOOM

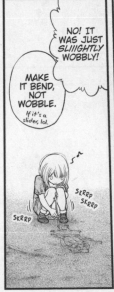

SKRRP SKRRP

SKRRP

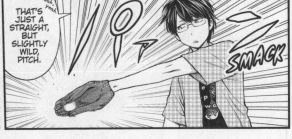

THAT'S JUST A STRAIGHT, BUT SLIGHTLY WILD, PITCH.

Yeah, yeah.

SMACK

ONIICHAN! I DREW IT REALLY GOOD!
SWING
YEAH, LATER!
BWOOSH
HYPER-ATOMIC ECCENTRIC FORK!
SLAP
AND THAT WAS JUST A WEAK AND UNCON-TROLLED STRAIGHT BALL.
NO WAY! LIKE I SAID, IT WOBBLES, JUST A LITTLE!
I TOLD YOU NOT TO MAKE IT WOBBLE!
MAKE IT FALL IF IT'S A FORK!
lol!
...
Hup!
ZOOM
WHOOPS!
BOP
WHAT'RE YOU DOING? YOU SUCK.
SHUT UP, JERK!
BOOOING
BOING

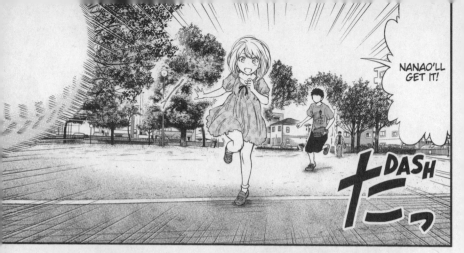

NANAO'LL GET IT!

DASH

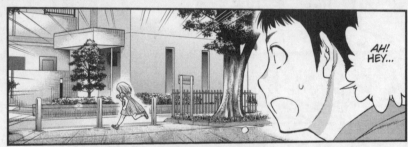

AH! HEY...

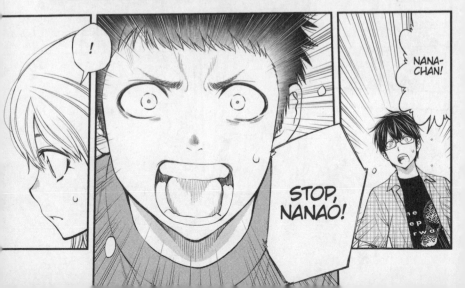

!

NANA-CHAN!

STOP, NANAO!

HUH?
SKREEEEEEEE
NANAOOOOOO!
SMACK

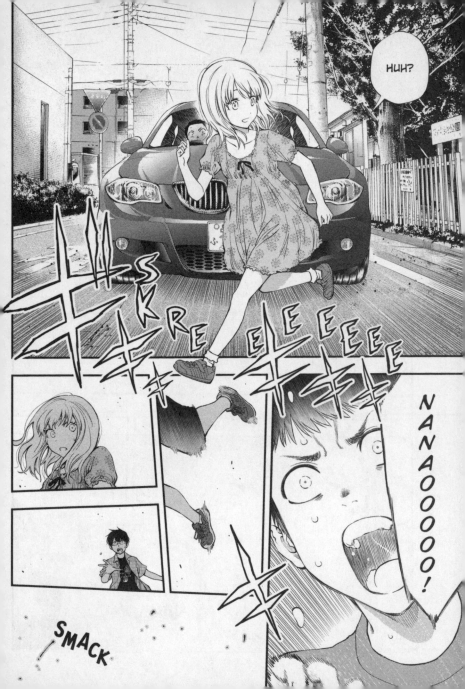

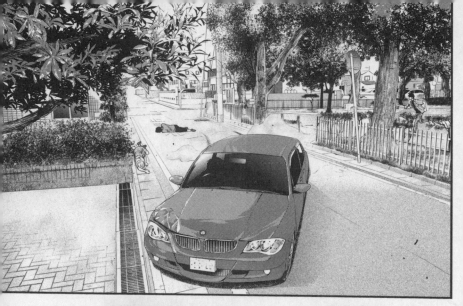

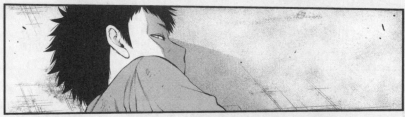

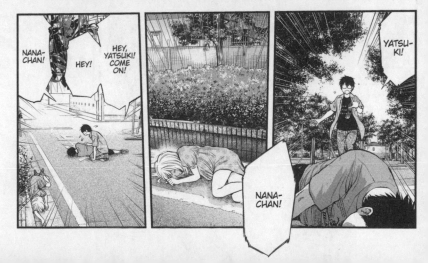

NANA-
CHAN!

HEY!

HEY,
YATSUKI!
COME
ON!

YATSU-
KI!

NANA-
CHAN!

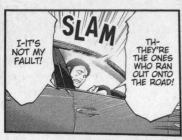

I-IT'S NOT MY FAULT!

SLAM

TH-THEY'RE THE ONES WHO RAN OUT ONTO THE ROAD!

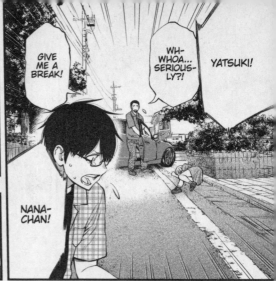

GIVE ME A BREAK!

WH-WHOA... SERIOUSLY?!

YATSUKI!

NANA-CHAN!

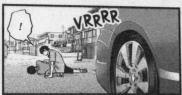

!

VRRRR

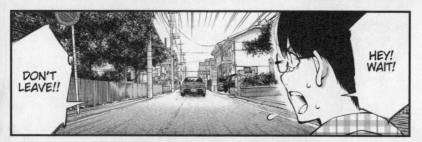

DON'T LEAVE!!

HEY! WAIT!

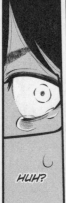

HUH?

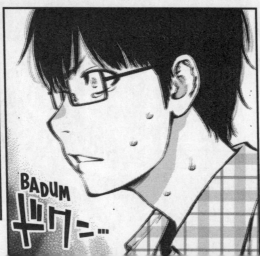

BADUM

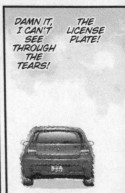

DAMN IT, I CAN'T SEE THROUGH THE TEARS!

THE LICENSE PLATE!

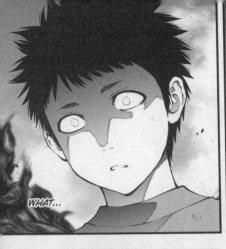

WHAT...

IS THAT...

YATSUKI?

WING?

BLACK...
FLAME...?

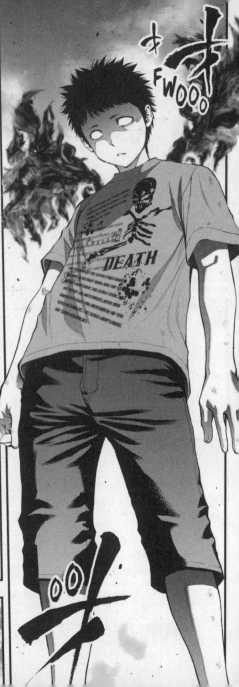

FWOOO

DEATH

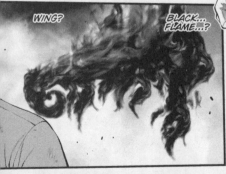

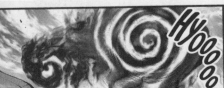

HYOOOO

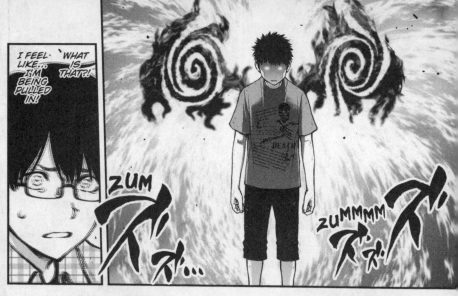

I FEEL LIKE... I'M BEING PULLED IN!

WHAT IS THAT?!

ZUM

ZUMMMM

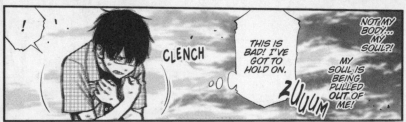

!

CLENCH

THIS IS BAD! I'VE GOT TO HOLD ON.

ZUUUM

NOT MY BODY!... MY SOUL?!

MY SOUL IS BEING PULLED OUT OF ME!

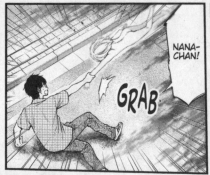

NANA-CHAN!

GRAB

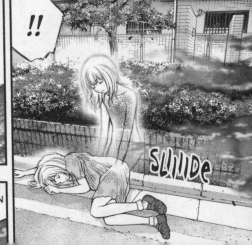

!!

SLIIIDE

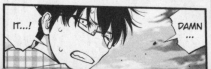

IT...!

DAMN...

STOP IT, YATSUKI!
WHAT ARE YOU DOING?! THAT'S NANA-CHAN!
IT'S YOUR SISTER!
STOP IT!!

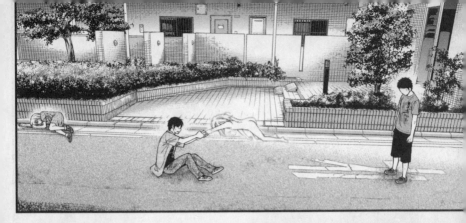

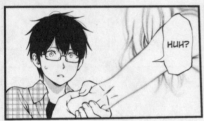

HUH?

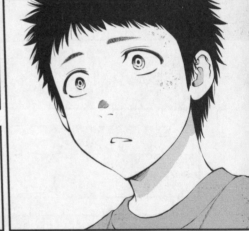

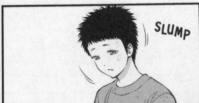

SLUMP

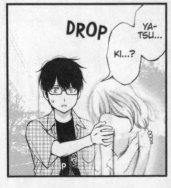

DROP

YA-TSU...

KI...?

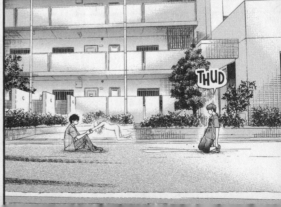

THUD

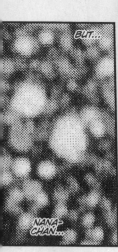

BUT...

NANA-CHAN...

HUH? HEY! WHAT'S HAPPENED TO YOU KIDS?!

NANA-CHAN!

HE WAS TAKEN TO THE HOSPITAL, BUT HE HAD NOTHING MORE THAN MINOR BRUISES AND SCRAPES.

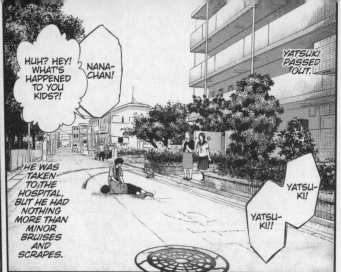

YATSUKI PASSED OUT.

YATSU-KI!

YATSU-KI!!

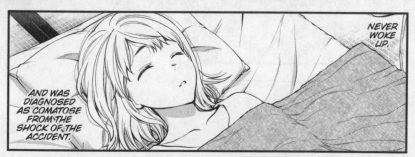

NEVER WOKE UP.

AND WAS DIAGNOSED AS COMATOSE FROM THE SHOCK OF THE ACCIDENT.

OF COURSE, NANA-CHAN DIDN'T REMEMBER THE INCIDENT, HAVING BEEN UNCONSCIOUS.

BUT YATSUKI DIDN'T REMEMBER IT, EITHER.

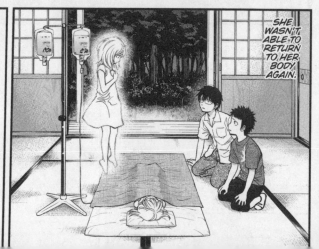

SHE WASN'T ABLE TO RETURN TO HER BODY AGAIN.

HE'S BEEN...

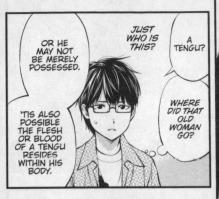

OR HE MAY NOT BE MERELY POSSESSED.

JUST WHO IS THIS?

A TENGU?

'TIS ALSO POSSIBLE THE FLESH OR BLOOD OF A TENGU RESIDES WITHIN HIS BODY.

WHERE DID THAT OLD WOMAN GO?

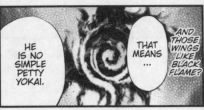

HE IS NO SIMPLE PETTY YOKAI.

THAT MEANS...

AND THOSE WINGS LIKE BLACK FLAME?

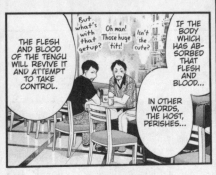

THE FLESH AND BLOOD OF THE TENGU WILL REVIVE IT AND ATTEMPT TO TAKE CONTROL.

But, what's with that getup?

Oh man! Those huge tits!

Isn't the cute?

IF THE BODY WHICH HAS AB-SORBED THAT FLESH AND BLOOD...

IN OTHER WORDS, THE HOST, PERISHES...

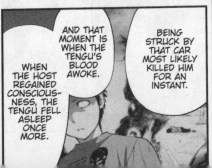

WHEN THE HOST REGAINED CONSCIOUS-NESS, THE TENGU FELL ASLEEP ONCE MORE.

AND THAT MOMENT IS WHEN THE TENGU'S BLOOD AWOKE.

BEING STRUCK BY THAT CAR MOST LIKELY KILLED HIM FOR AN INSTANT.

POSSESSED BY A TENGU.

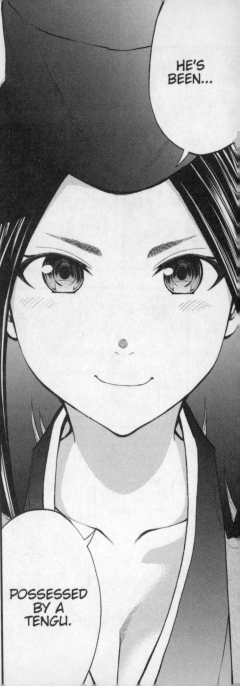

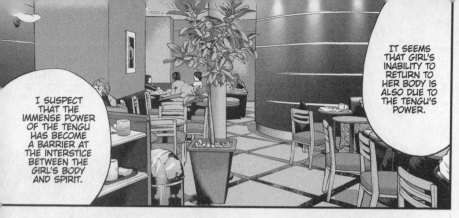

IT SEEMS THAT GIRL'S INABILITY TO RETURN TO HER BODY IS ALSO DUE TO THE TENGU'S POWER.

I SUSPECT THAT THE IMMENSE POWER OF THE TENGU HAS BECOME A BARRIER AT THE INTERSTICE BETWEEN THE GIRL'S BODY AND SPIRIT.

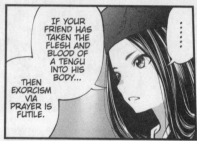

IF YOUR FRIEND HAS TAKEN THE FLESH AND BLOOD OF A TENGU INTO HIS BODY...

THEN EXORCISM VIA PRAYER IS FUTILE.

· · · · ·

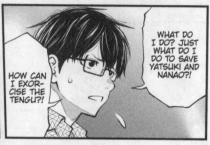

HOW CAN I EXORCISE THE TENGU?!

WHAT DO I DO? JUST WHAT DO I DO TO SAVE YATSUKI AND NANAO?!

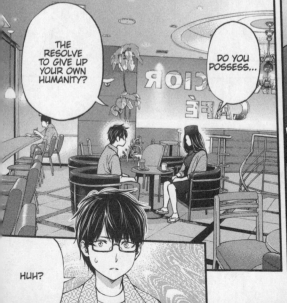

THE RESOLVE TO GIVE UP YOUR OWN HUMANITY?

DO YOU POSSESS...

HUH?

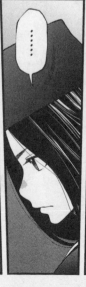

· · · · ·

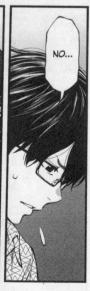

NO...

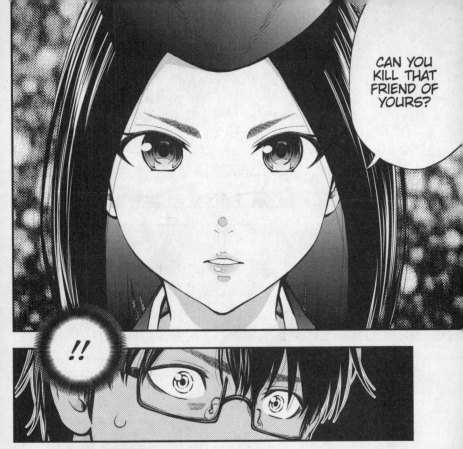

CAN YOU KILL THAT FRIEND OF YOURS?

!!

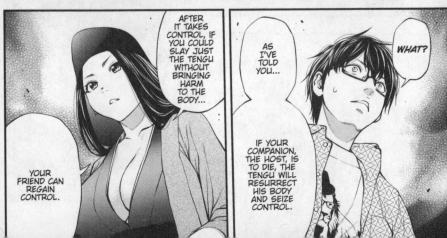

AFTER IT TAKES CONTROL, IF YOU COULD SLAY JUST THE TENGU WITHOUT BRINGING HARM TO THE BODY...

AS I'VE TOLD YOU...

WHAT?

YOUR FRIEND CAN REGAIN CONTROL.

IF YOUR COMPANION, THE HOST, IS TO DIE, THE TENGU WILL RESURRECT HIS BODY AND SEIZE CONTROL.

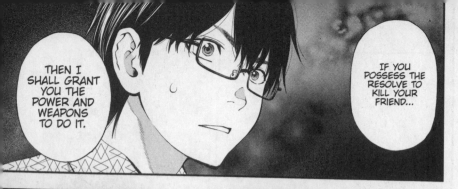

THEN I SHALL GRANT YOU THE POWER AND WEAPONS TO DO IT.

IF YOU POSSESS THE RESOLVE TO KILL YOUR FRIEND...

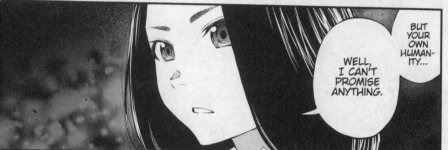

BUT YOUR OWN HUMANITY...

WELL, I CAN'T PROMISE ANYTHING.

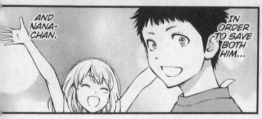

AND NANA-CHAN.

IN ORDER TO SAVE BOTH HIM...

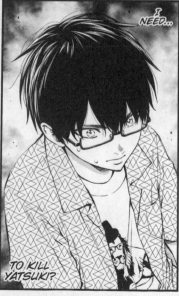

I NEED...

TO KILL YATSUKI?

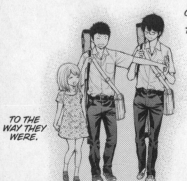

IN ORDER TO RETURN THINGS...

TO THE WAY THEY WERE.

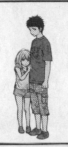

I DON'T CARE IF NANA-CHAN HATES ME, EITHER.

EVEN IF YATSUKI ENDS UP HATING ME FOR IT, THAT'S FINE.

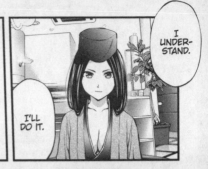

I UNDERSTAND.

I'LL DO IT.

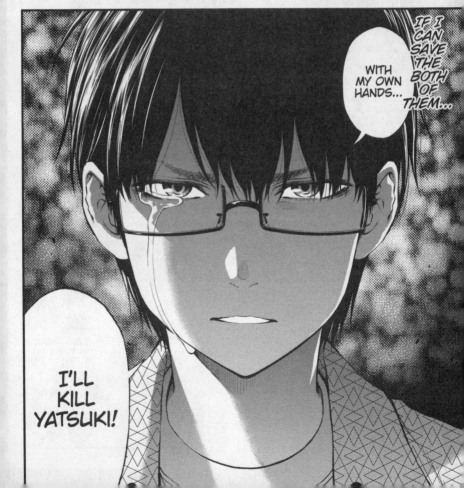

IF I CAN SAVE THE BOTH OF THEM...

WITH MY OWN HANDS...

I'LL KILL YATSUKI!

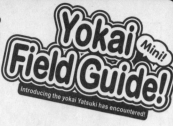

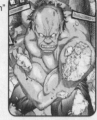 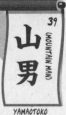

39 山男 (MOUNTAIN MAN)

YAMAOTOKO

Written with the kanji for "mountain" and "height," this yokai is said to appear in mountainous regions of Japan. They're often said to have a kind nature.

First appears in chapter 135

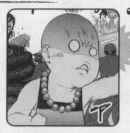 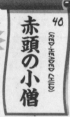

40 赤頭の小僧 (RED-HEADED CHILD)

AKA-ATAMA NO KOZOU

Once there was a man named Aka-atama who took pride in his strength. When he was resting in a temple of Kanon, a local child of about four or five drew near. They began to play by driving spikes of about five *sun* (one *sun* is about three cm) in and out of the temple pillars. If Aka-atama used both hands, he could drive the spikes in, but he couldn't get them out. It's said when the child saw this, he walked off, laughing.

First appears in chapter 135

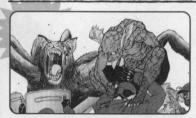 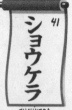

41 ショウケラ

SHOUKERA

This yokai is related to the Koshin faith. It's said to observe whether people are living righteously, and if they're doing evil, it gouges at their insides with its sharp claws.

First appears in chapter 135

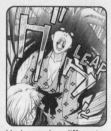 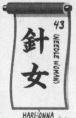

43 針女 (NEEDLE WOMAN)

HARI-ONNA

Hari-onna is a different name for the nure-joshi, and stories of it are passed down in Uwajima in Ehime prefecture. A yokai in the form of a woman with wild hair, she smiles at passing men, and when a man smiles back, she can possess him.

First appears in chapter chapter 139

42 土蜘蛛 (EARTH SPIDER)

TSUCHIGUMO

Said to have the head of an oni, the body of a tiger, and long spider legs, these yokai live in the mountains; they immobilize travelers with their thread and devour them.

First appears in chapter 135

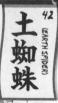 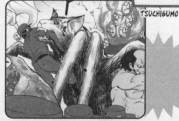

139
We Have A Deal! ♪

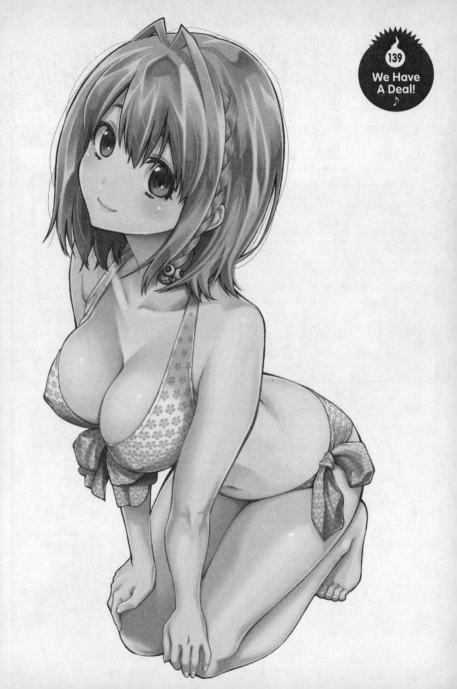

I REMEMBERED EVERYTHING.

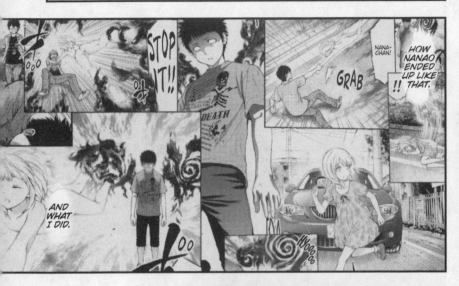

STOP IT!!

NANA-CHAN!

GRAB

HOW NANAO ENDED UP LIKE THAT.

AND WHAT I DID.

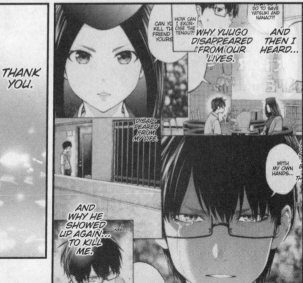

SO...

THANK YOU.

THAT'S...

ENOUGH.

I'LL...

CAN YOU KILL THE FRIEND YOURS—

HOW CAN I EXORCISE THE TENGU?!

WHY YUUGO DISAPPEARED FROM OUR LIVES.

TO DO TO SAVE YATSUKI AND NANAO?!

AND THEN I HEARD...

DISAP-PEARED FROM MY LIFE.

WITH MY OWN HANDS...

AND WHY HE SHOWED UP AGAIN... TO KILL ME.

PUT EVERYTHING I HAVE INTO STOPPING YOU, TOO!
FWOOO
OPEN YOUR EYES, YUUGO!
HOTTEST UNDERGROUND IDOLS DAILY PERFORMANCE

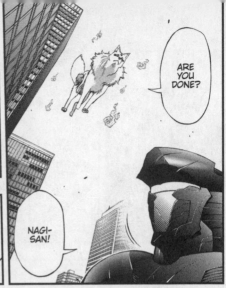

ARE YOU DONE?

I HOPE THIS WILL BRING HIM BACK.

YEAH! I'VE BROKEN OFF HIS HORN, THE SOURCE OF HIS ONI POWER.

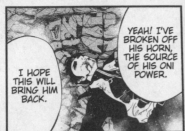

YEAH, I'M DONE.

FWUMP

WAIT, SO WHAT ABOUT YOU, NAGI-SAN--

NAGI-SAN!

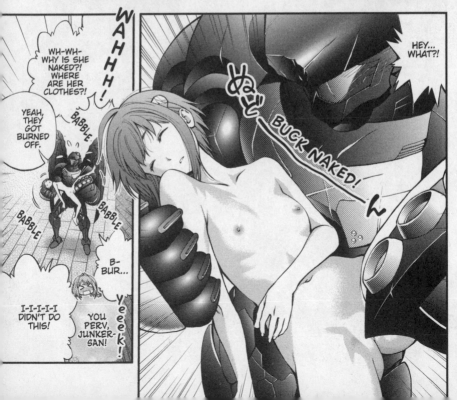

WAHHH!

HEY... WHAT?!

WH-WH-WHY IS SHE NAKED?! WHERE ARE HER CLOTHES?!

ぬぐ BUCK NAKED! ん

YEAH, THEY GOT BURNED OFF.

BABBLE

BABBLE

BABBLE

BABBLE

B-BUR...

YEEEK!

I-I-I-I-I DIDN'T DO THIS!

YOU PERV, JUNKER-SAN!

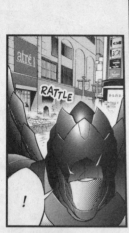

RATTLE

!

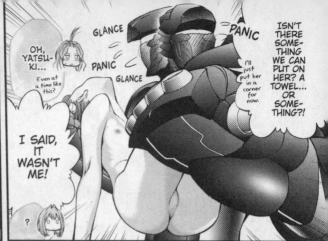

GLANCE

PANIC

GLANCE

OH, YATSU-KI...

Even at a time like this?

I'll just put her in a corner for now.

I SAID, IT WASN'T ME!

?

PANIC

ISN'T THERE SOME-THING WE CAN PUT ON HER? A TOWEL... OR SOME-THING?!

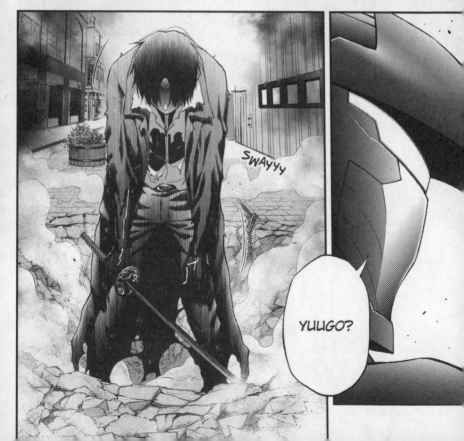

SWAYYY

YUUGO?

uo
ARGH!
GYAH!
DAMN IT! I'M ALMOST OUT OF LTP GAS!
UAGH!
DOES ANYONE HAVE ANY?!
I'M RUNNING OUT OF AMMO, TOO!
BAM
THERE'S NO END TO THEM!
BA-BLAM

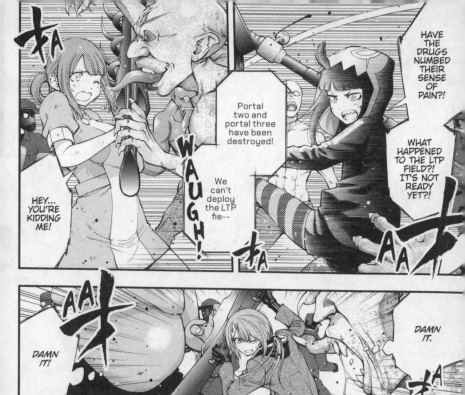

HAVE THE DRUGS NUMBED THEIR SENSE OF PAIN?!

Portal two and portal three have been destroyed!

WHAT HAPPENED TO THE LTP FIELD?! IT'S NOT READY YET?!

We can't deploy the LTP fie--

HEY... YOU'RE KIDDING ME!

DAMN IT!

DAMN IT.

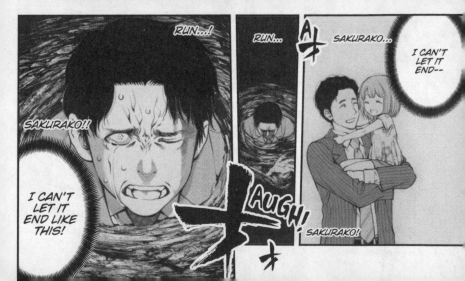

RUN...!

RUN...

SAKURAKO...

I CAN'T LET IT END--

SAKURAKO!!

I CAN'T LET IT END LIKE THIS!

SAKURAKO!

!!
YUKIMURA-KUN, BEHIND YOU!
!!
LEAP
CRAP.

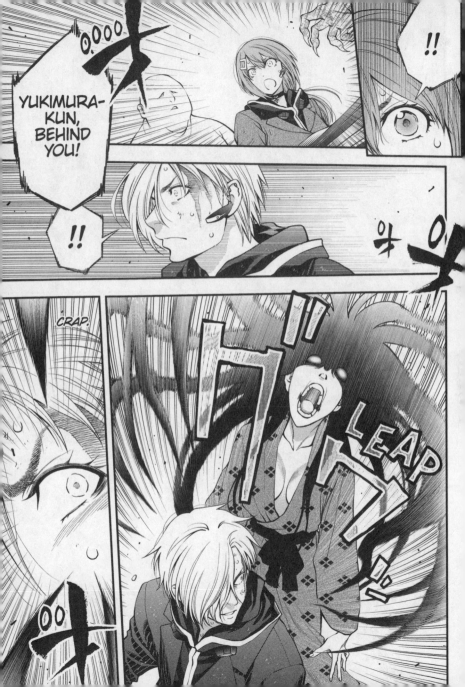

SLAM

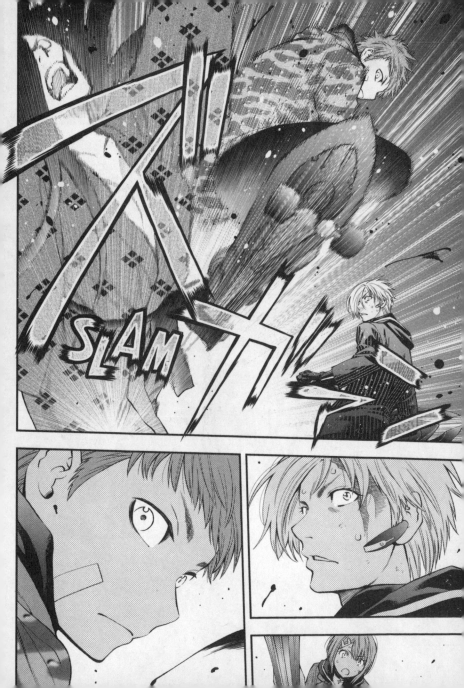

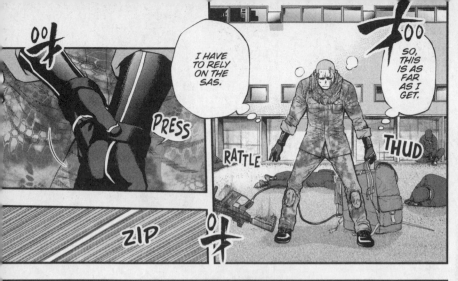

I HAVE TO RELY ON THE SAS.

SO, THIS IS AS FAR AS I GET.

PRESS

RATTLE

THUD

ZIP

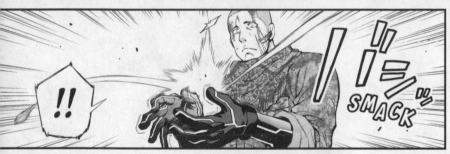

!!

SMACK

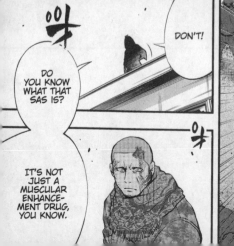

DON'T!

DO YOU KNOW WHAT THAT SAS IS?

IT'S NOT JUST A MUSCULAR ENHANCE-MENT DRUG, YOU KNOW.

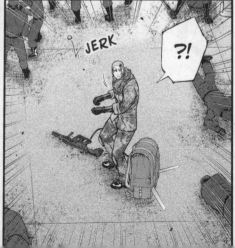

JERK

?!

IT'S MADE BY REFINING THE BLOOD OF THE YOKAI YOU ALL HATE SO MUCH!
IN OTHER WORDS, THAT DRUG WILL TURN YOU INTO A HALF-YOKAI.
IF YOU DON'T WANT TO END UP LIKE THAT GIRL DEN-POUYA...
...!
THEN YOU'D BEST FORGET ABOUT IT!
......
RIN...

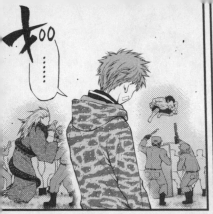

DIDN'T YOU BETRAY US?

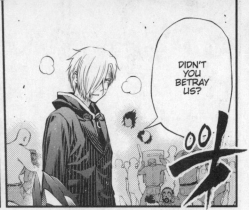

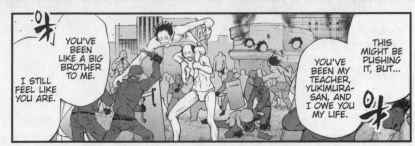

YOU'VE BEEN LIKE A BIG BROTHER TO ME.

I STILL FEEL LIKE YOU ARE.

YOU'VE BEEN MY TEACHER, YUKIMURA-SAN, AND I OWE YOU MY LIFE.

THIS MIGHT BE PUSHING IT, BUT...

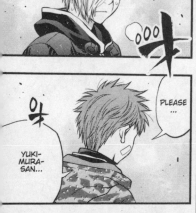

PLEASE...

YUKI-MURA-SAN...

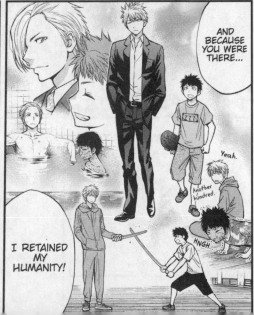

AND BECAUSE YOU WERE THERE...

Yeah.

Another hundred.

HNGH

I RETAINED MY HUMANITY!

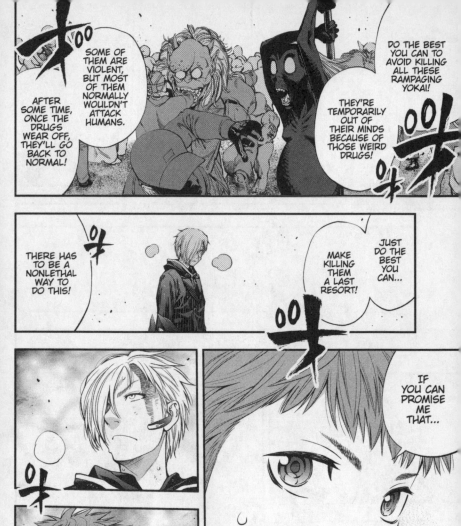

SOME OF THEM ARE VIOLENT, BUT MOST OF THEM NORMALLY WOULDN'T ATTACK HUMANS.

AFTER SOME TIME, ONCE THE DRUGS WEAR OFF, THEY'LL GO BACK TO NORMAL!

DO THE BEST YOU CAN TO AVOID KILLING ALL THESE RAMPAGING YOKAI!

THEY'RE TEMPORARILY OUT OF THEIR MINDS BECAUSE OF THOSE WEIRD DRUGS!

THERE HAS TO BE A NONLETHAL WAY TO DO THIS!

MAKE KILLING THEM A LAST RESORT!

JUST DO THE BEST YOU CAN...

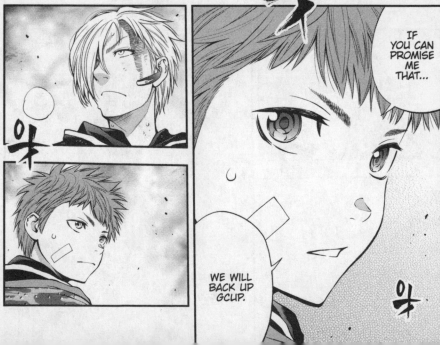

IF YOU CAN PROMISE ME THAT...

WE WILL BACK UP GCUP.

YUKIMURA-KUN...
YUKIMURA-SAN...
PLEASE!
YUKIMURA-SAN...
NO...
GYAH!
......
ARGH!
I THOUGHT OF YOU AS A CHEEKY LITTLE BROTHER.
BUT I NEVER IMAGINED YOU'D COME TELL ME TO BEND MY FUNDAMENTAL IDEALS.

YOU'RE ALL LISTENING, AREN'T YOU?
WE'LL ACCEPT THEIR DEMAND!
!
AVOID KILLING NES WHENEVER POSSIBLE!
NONLETHAL TACTICS AND AMMUNITION! CAPTURE THEM IF YOU CAN!
RIGHT!
GUESS WE GOTTA!
ROGER.
WE HAVE...

A DEAL!!
KRRRAK
KA-BOOM
!
SHLOOP
TO THINK...
LOOM
THE DAY WOULD COME WHEN I WOULD JOIN HANDS WITH YOU!

MOVE, MOVE, YOU PETTY PEONS!
HYOOO HYO HYO
YOU PISSANTS THINK YOU'RE A MATCH FOR ME?!
SPINNING KAKICK!
THWAK
WAK WAK WAK WAK WAK
SHHHHHRIP!
KAPPA THE RIPPER!
SLICE!
HERE AH COME!
WOOSH
EXTREME WHEEL OF PURGATORY!

KTAM
TAM
TAM

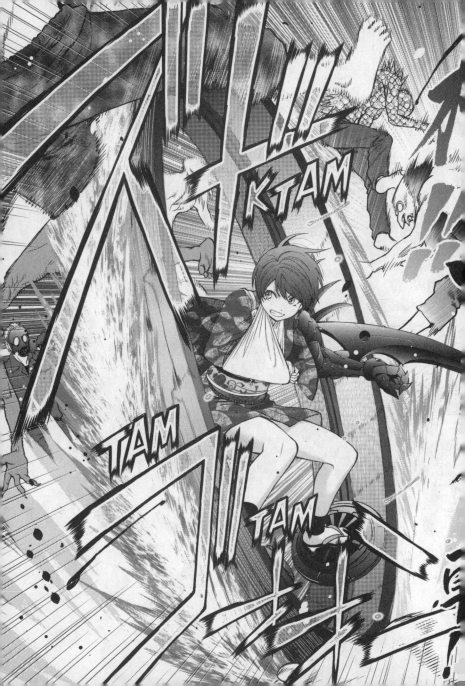

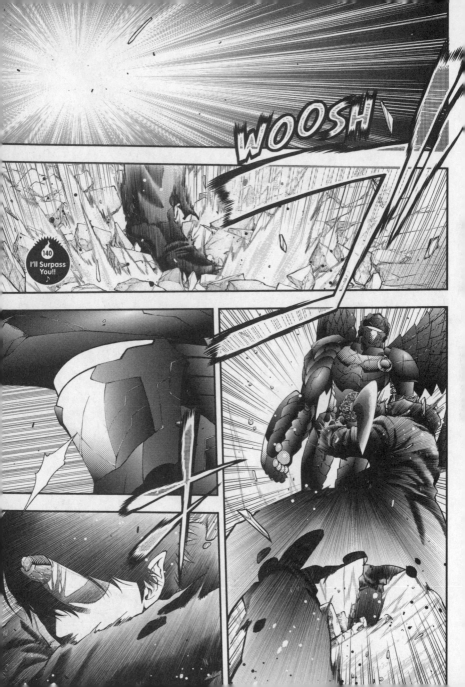

WOOSH

140
I'll Surpass You!! ♪

140
I'll Surpass You!! ♪
BAM!!

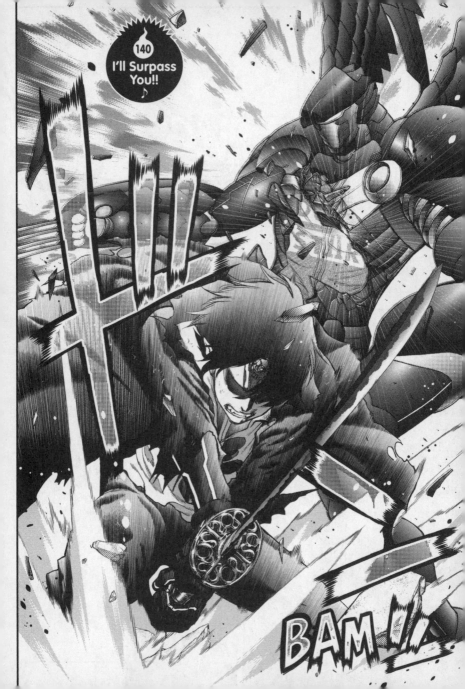

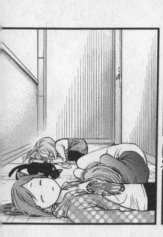

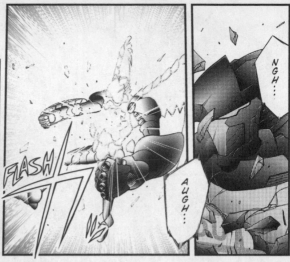

FLASH

NGH...

AUGH...

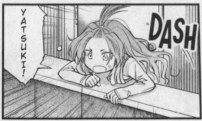

YATSUKI!

DASH

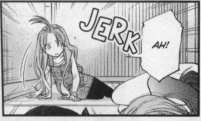

JERK

AH!

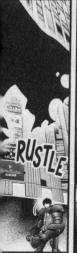

RUSTLE

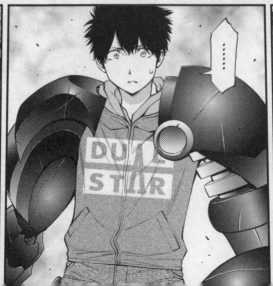

DUAL STAR

・・・・・

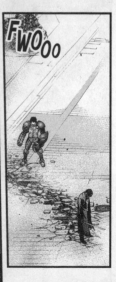

FWOOO

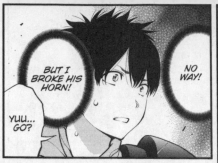

NO WAY!

BUT I BROKE HIS HORN!

YUU... GO?

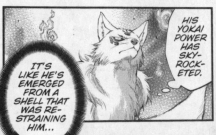

HIS YOKAI POWER HAS SKY-ROCK-ETED.

IT'S LIKE HE'S EMERGED FROM A SHELL THAT WAS RE-STRAINING HIM...

RELEASING HIS TRUE, UNSHACKLED POWER!

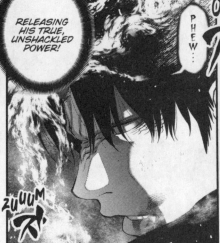

PHEW...

OOze

ZUUUM

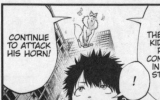

CONTINUE TO ATTACK HIS HORN!

YATSUKI! THE FACT THAT KIDOUMARU'S POWER IS CONCENTRATED IN HIS HORN STILL HOLDS TRUE!

!

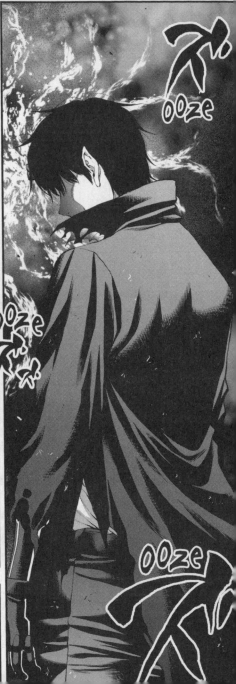

OOze

OOze

OOze

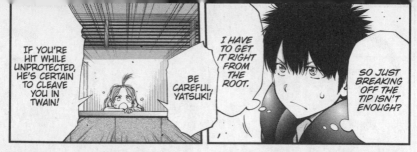

IF YOU'RE HIT WHILE UNPROTECTED, HE'S CERTAIN TO CLEAVE YOU IN TWAIN!

BE CAREFUL, YATSUKI!

I HAVE TO GET IT RIGHT FROM THE ROOT.

SO JUST BREAKING OFF THE TIP ISN'T ENOUGH?

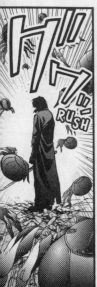

ゴゴゴ
RUSH

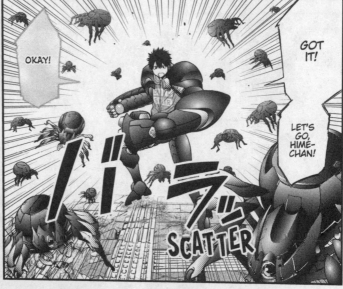

OKAY!

GOT IT!

LET'S GO, HIMÉ-CHAN!

バラ
SCATTER

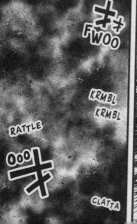

キ
FWOO

KRMBL
KRMBL

RATTLE

000キ

CLATTA

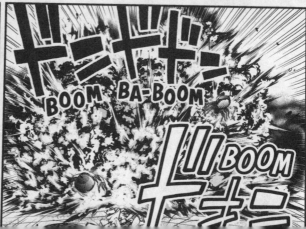

ドドドドン
BOOM BA-BOOM

ドリリBOOM

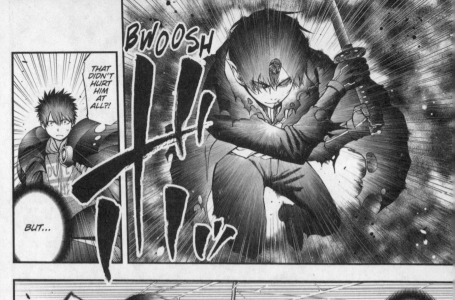

BWOOSH

THAT DIDN'T HURT HIM AT ALL?!

BUT...

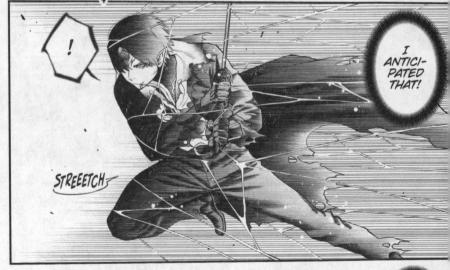

!

STREEETCH

I ANTICI-PATED THAT!

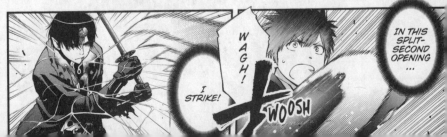

WAGH! I STRIKE!

WOOSH

IN THIS SPLIT-SECOND OPENING ...

GA-TAM
WHA...?
HE COMPLETELY POWERED THROUGH...
HIME-CHAN'S THREAD!
JERK
HONEY!
HIME!
FLASH
BAM
WOOSH
KUH...

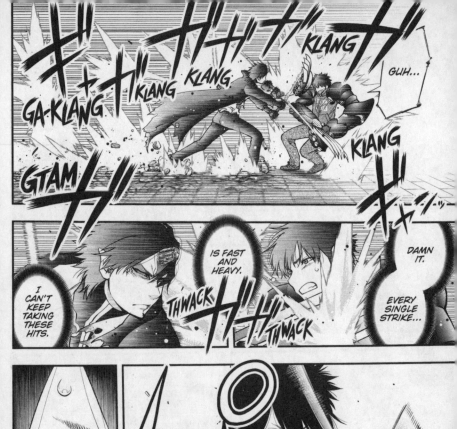

GUH...

I CAN'T KEEP TAKING THESE HITS.

IS FAST AND HEAVY.

DAMN IT.

EVERY SINGLE STRIKE...

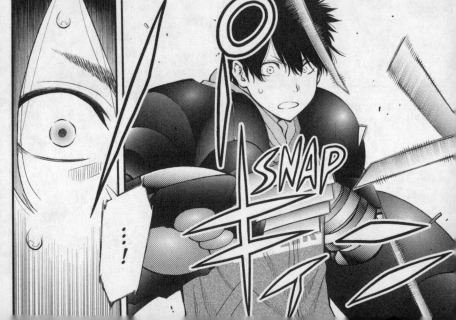

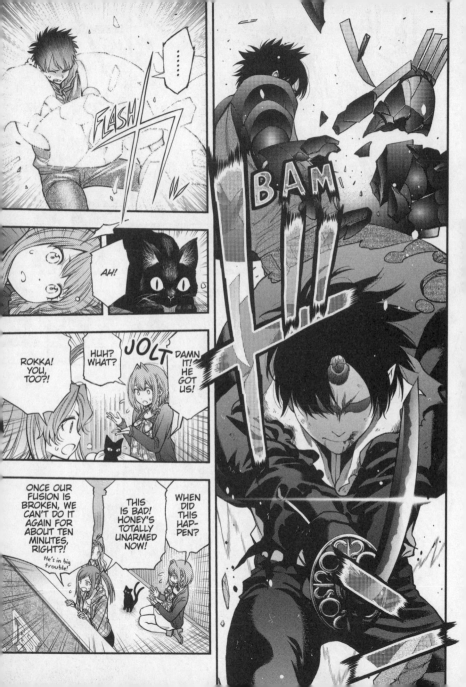

......

FLASH

BAM!!!

AH!

ROKKA! YOU, TOO?!

HUH? WHAT?

JOLT

DAMN IT! HE GOT US!

ONCE OUR FUSION IS BROKEN, WE CAN'T DO IT AGAIN FOR ABOUT TEN MINUTES, RIGHT?!

He's in big trouble!

THIS IS BAD! HONEY'S TOTALLY UNARMED NOW!

WHEN DID THIS HAP-PEN?

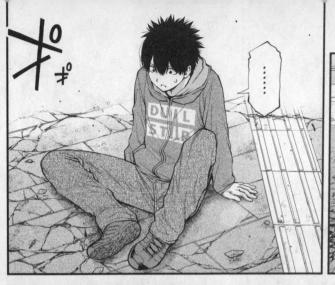

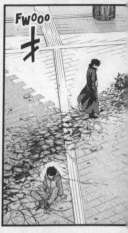

FWOOO

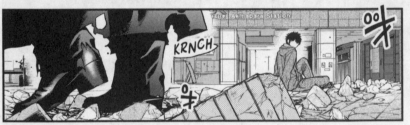

Akihabara Station

KRNCH

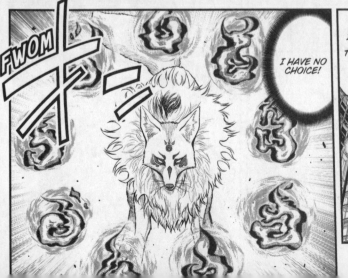

FWOM

I HAVE NO CHOICE!

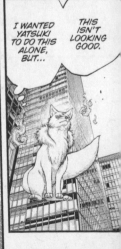

I WANTED YATSUKI TO DO THIS ALONE, BUT...

THIS ISN'T LOOKING GOOD.

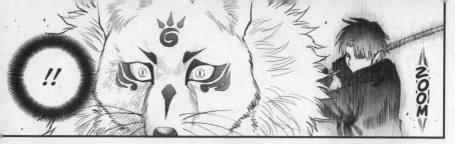

!!

ZOOM

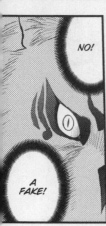

NO!

A FAKE!

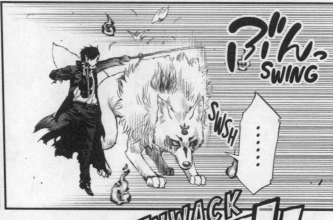

ぶん〜 SWING

SWSH

....

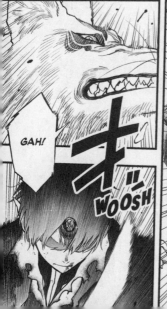

GAH!

WOOSH

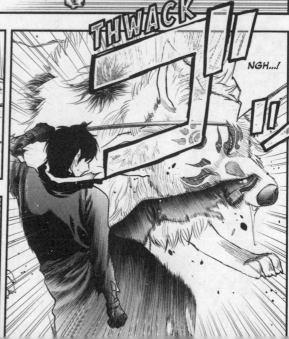

THWACK

NGH...!

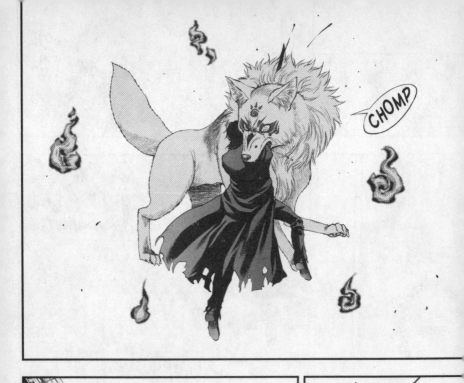

CHOMP

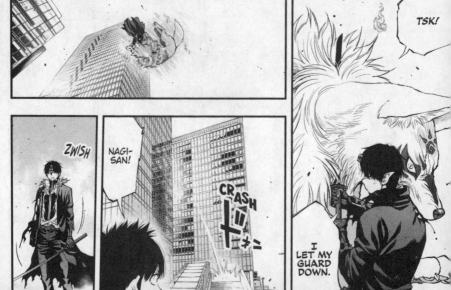

TSK!

ZWISH

NAGI-
SAN!

CRASH

I LET MY
GUARD
DOWN.

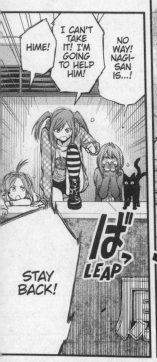

HIME! I CAN'T TAKE IT! I'M GOING TO HELP HIM! NO WAY! NAGI-SAN IS...!

STAY BACK!

ば、LEAP

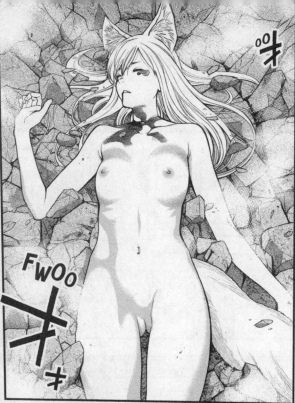

FWOO

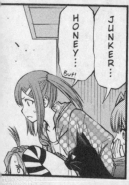

HONEY... JUNKER... But!

I'VE BEEN SO USELESS. SORRY, NAGI-SAN.

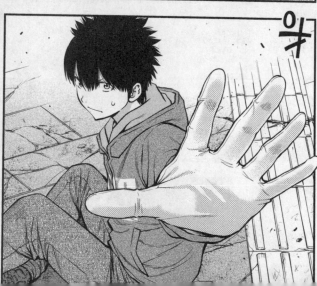

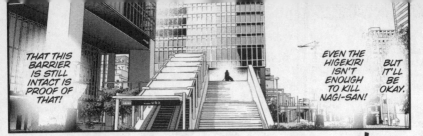

THAT THIS BARRIER IS STILL INTACT IS PROOF OF THAT!

EVEN THE HIGEKIRI ISN'T ENOUGH TO KILL NAGI-SAN!

BUT IT'LL BE OKAY.

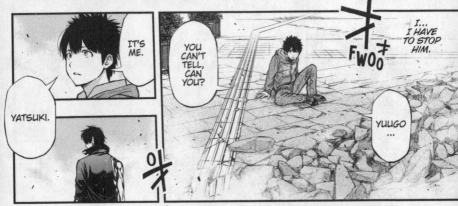

IT'S ME.

YOU CAN'T TELL, CAN YOU?

YATSUKI.

I... I HAVE TO STOP HIM.

FWOO

YUUGO...

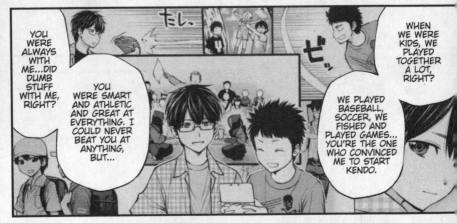

YOU WERE ALWAYS WITH ME...DID DUMB STUFF WITH ME, RIGHT?

YOU WERE SMART AND ATHLETIC AND GREAT AT EVERYTHING. I COULD NEVER BEAT YOU AT ANYTHING, BUT...

WHEN WE WERE KIDS, WE PLAYED TOGETHER A LOT, RIGHT?

WE PLAYED BASEBALL, SOCCER, WE FISHED AND PLAYED GAMES... YOU'RE THE ONE WHO CONVINCED ME TO START KENDO.

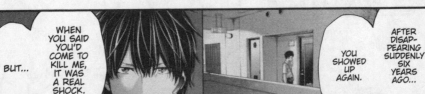

WHEN YOU SAID YOU'D COME TO KILL ME, IT WAS A REAL SHOCK.

BUT...

YOU SHOWED UP AGAIN.

AFTER DISAPPEARING SUDDENLY SIX YEARS AGO...

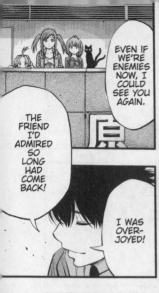

EVEN IF WE'RE ENEMIES NOW, I COULD SEE YOU AGAIN.

THE FRIEND I'D ADMIRED SO LONG HAD COME BACK!

I WAS OVERJOYED!

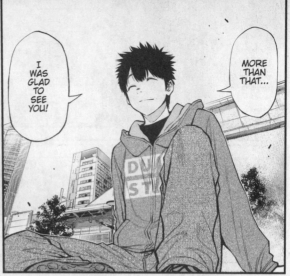

I WAS GLAD TO SEE YOU!

MORE THAN THAT...

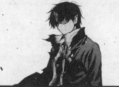

I WANT TO SAVE YOU *JUST AS MUCH* AS YOU WANTED TO SAVE ME.

BUT THIS IS THE ONE TIME I WON'T LOSE.

I NEVER BEAT YOU IN ANYTHING.

I'M GOING TO SURPASS YOU.

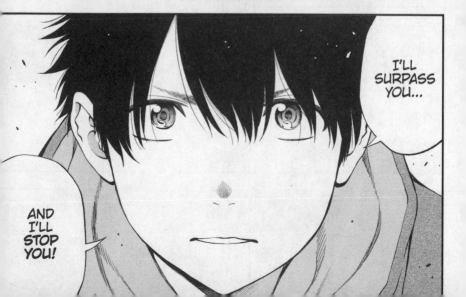

I'LL SURPASS YOU...

AND I'LL STOP YOU!

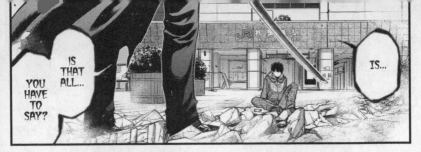

YOU HAVE TO SAY?

IS THAT ALL...

IS...

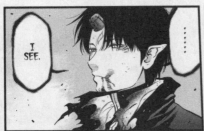

I SEE.

.....

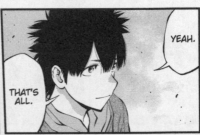

YEAH.

THAT'S ALL.

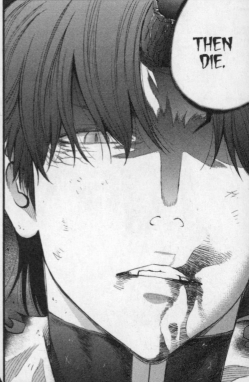

THEN DIE.

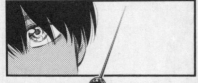

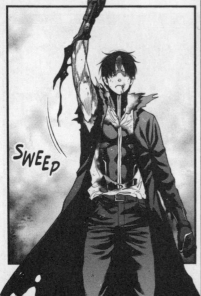

SWEEP

THIS IS IT!
ROKKA!
COME!
KAAAH

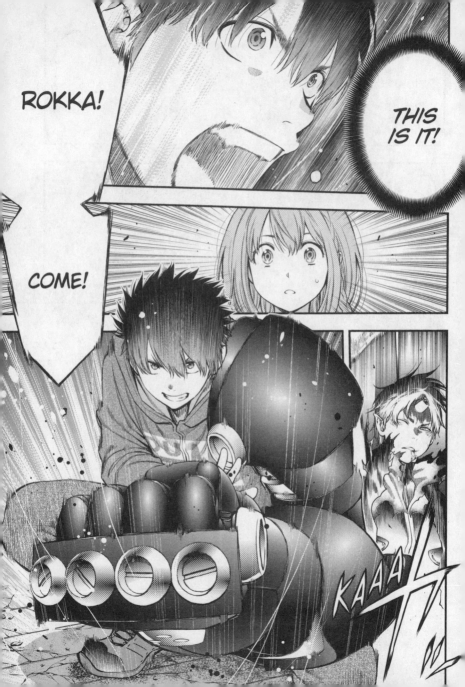

BAM

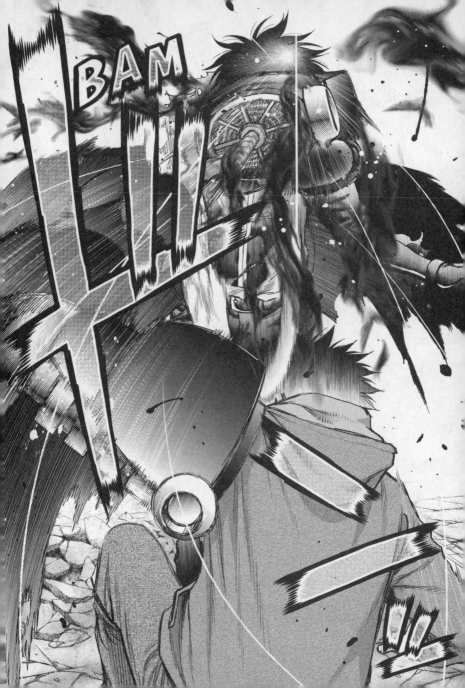

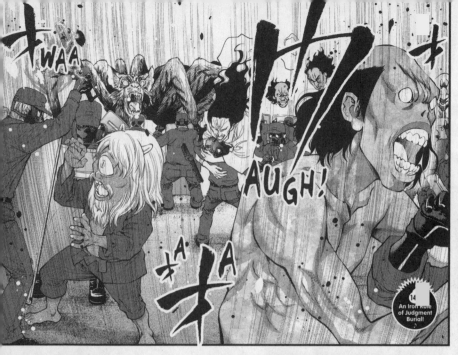

An Iron Rule of Judgment Burial!

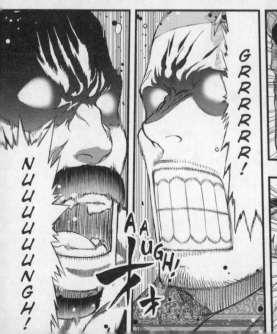

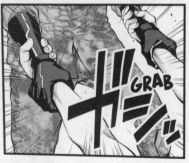

GRAB

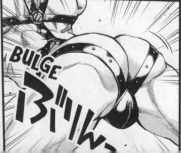

BULGE

141
An Iron Rule of Judgment Burial! ♪
大回転甘尻大竜巻ッ!!!!
GREAT SPINNING SWEET-ASSED TORNADO!
WHIRLY
SWIRLY
WHIRL
WHIRLY
Sweet...!

ARC JET BULLET!
ZA-TAM
極煉獄業車輪!!!!!
EXTREME WHEEL OF PURGATORY!

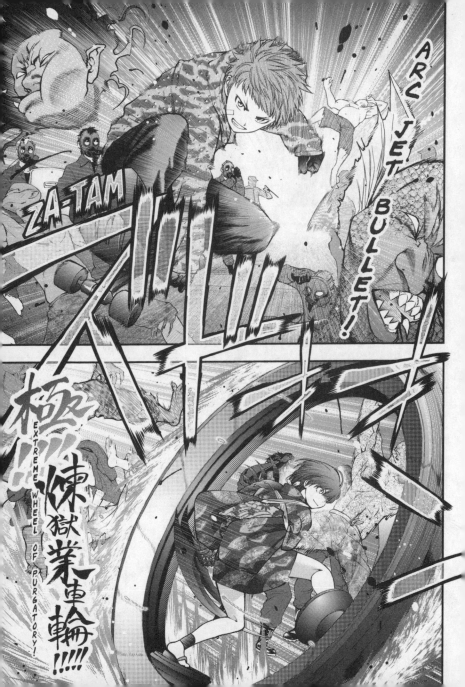

WOW!
THEY MAKE GREAT ALLIES!
RAAT
DUH!
THWACK
SHE'S THE ONLY ONE I COULDN'T KILL.
SHE'S GOTTA BE AT LEAST THAT STRONG!
HSSS!
PUSHHH
TEE HEE! ♪
DON'T GIGGLE OVER THIS! I'LL RIP OFF YOUR USELESS BITS!
THEY'RE NOT USE-LESS!
HYAHH!
TOSS
Boobs!
Boobs!
TRUE, THEY'RE GOOD TOOLS FOR LURING IN STUPID MEN.
THEY LURE IN SMART MEN, TOO!
Not that I've ever caught any.
GYUUUGYUUU
AGH! ONE STRIKE'S TUCKERED ME OUT.
You can't beat age.
Do your best, kids!
No females...
DSHOOO
AAGH!
WHERE IS IT?!
SWOOSH

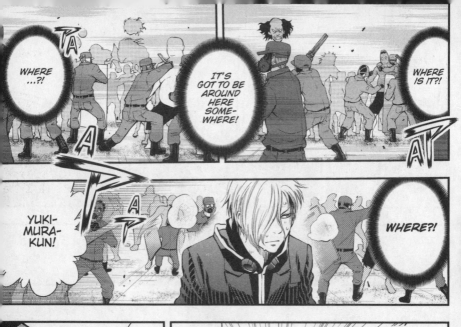

WHERE...?!

IT'S GOT TO BE AROUND HERE SOMEWHERE!

WHERE IS IT?!

YUKI-MURA-KUN!

WHERE?!

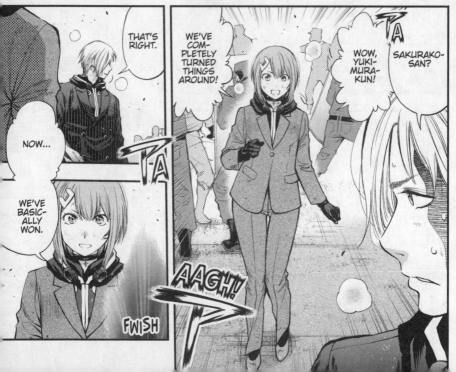

THAT'S RIGHT.

WE'VE COMPLETELY TURNED THINGS AROUND!

WOW, YUKI-MURA-KUN!

SAKURAKO-SAN?

NOW...

WE'VE BASICALLY WON.

AAGH!

FWISH

LEAN
SWIPE
!!
YOU'RE TOO FAR.
ONE METER, TWELVE CENTI-METERS, AND FIVE MILLI-METERS.
IF YOU WANT TO HIT ME...
YOU NEED TO BE WITHIN THAT RANGE.
I DIDN'T THINK IT WOULD COME TO ME.
YOU TAUGHT ME THAT, DIDN'T YOU...
OOZE

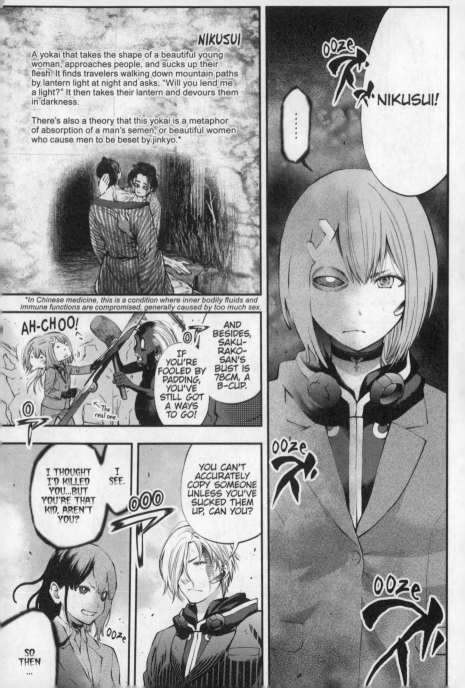

NIKUSUI

A yokai that takes the shape of a beautiful young woman, approaches people, and sucks up their flesh. It finds travelers walking down mountain paths by lantern light at night and asks, "Will you lend me a light?" It then takes their lantern and devours them in darkness.

There's also a theory that this yokai is a metaphor of absorption of a man's semen, or beautiful women who cause men to be beset by jinkyo.*

*In Chinese medicine, this is a condition where inner bodily fluids and immune functions are compromised, generally caused by too much sex.

WOULD YOU PREFER THIS INSTEAD...
YUKIMURA-KUN?
KUNO-SAN...
......
YOU'RE ALL GROWN UP, HUH?
A SUIT...
LOOKS GOOD ON YOU.
A NIKUSUI ABSORBS EVEN THE MEMORIES OF HER VICTIMS.
AGH! DAMN IT!

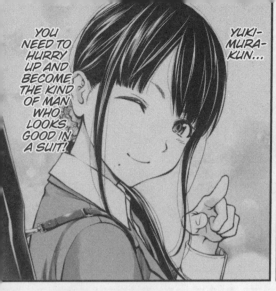

YOU NEED TO HURRY UP AND BECOME THE KIND OF MAN WHO LOOKS GOOD IN A SUIT!

YUKI-MURA-KUN...

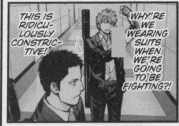

THIS IS RIDICU-LOUSLY CONSTRIC-TIVE!

WHY'RE WE WEARING SUITS WHEN WE'RE GOING TO BE FIGHTING?!

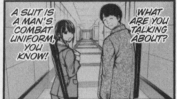

A SUIT IS A MAN'S COMBAT UNIFORM, YOU KNOW!

WHAT ARE YOU TALKING ABOUT?

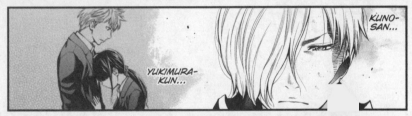

YUKIMURA-KUN...

KUNO-SAN...

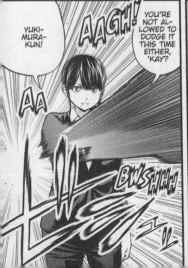

YUKI-MURA-KUN!

AAGH!

YOU'RE NOT AL-LOWED TO DODGE IT THIS TIME EITHER, 'KAY?

AA

BWSHH

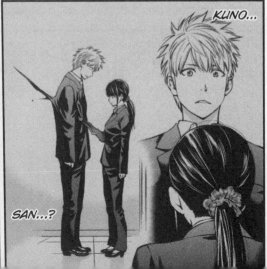

KUNO...

SAN...?

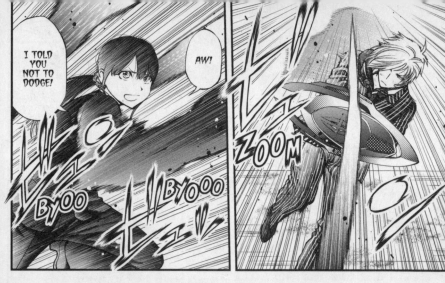

I TOLD YOU NOT TO DODGE!

AW!

ZOOM

BYOO

BYOOO

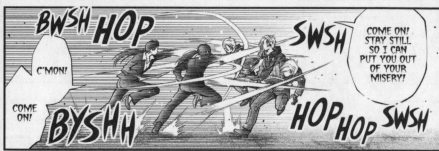

BWSH HOP

C'MON!

COME ON!

BYSHH

SWSH

COME ON! STAY STILL SO I CAN PUT YOU OUT OF YOUR MISERY!

HOP HOP SWSH

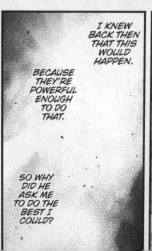

I KNEW BACK THEN THAT THIS WOULD HAPPEN.

BECAUSE THEY'RE POWERFUL ENOUGH TO DO THAT.

SO WHY DID HE ASK ME TO DO THE BEST I COULD?

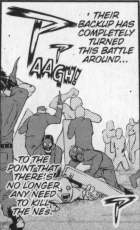

' THEIR BACKUP HAS COMPLETELY TURNED THIS BATTLE AROUND...

PAAGH!!

TO THE POINT THAT THERE'S NO LONGER ANY NEED TO KILL THE NES.

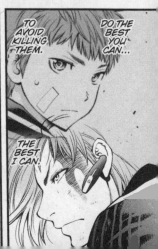

TO AVOID KILLING THEM.

DO THE BEST YOU CAN...

THE BEST I CAN.

AAA
KLING
GSHING
IF...
RAA
KLING
THE NOUMA THAT KILLED MY SISTER WERE HERE...
I'D KILL IT.
A
A
AS LONG AS THE NIKUSUI WHO KILLED KUNO-SAN IS HERE...
I COULDN'T TELL HIM NOT TO KILL ANY OF THEM.
YUKIMURA-SAN!
GET REVENGE FOR HER.
SWIF
SWIF
!
NGH!
TWITCH
AAGH!
GUH...

TA
GUGH...
SLUMP
GAH!
!
RAA
AGH...
AA
WHAT?
THE NIKUSUI IS...
YOU... BITCH.
IT'S IN PAIN?!
NN... GUH.
AAA
YUKI... MURAKU...
DO IT... NOW.
KILL... ME...
SQUEEZE
AA
NO WAY! KUNO-SAN?! IT'S NOT JUST HER MEMORIES AND FLESH THAT WERE ABORBED...
BUT HER SOUL ITSELF?!
AGH!
...MURAKU...
HURRY.

AUUT
YUKIMURA-SAN...?
HUR...
RY...
PU
......
WH--
WHY?
YOU MEAN YOU DON'T NEED MY HELP?
PU
YEAH.
UT
YOU'VE...
GROWN STRONG... YUKIMURA-KUN.
UT
I CAN'T... DO... ANY MORE THAN THIS...
UUGH!
PLEASE... YUKIMURA-KUN...
BEFORE IT'S OVER...

KISS...
ME.
AAA
AUGH!
You're Yukimura Junsei-kun?
Well, you're pretty good.
But not quite there yet!

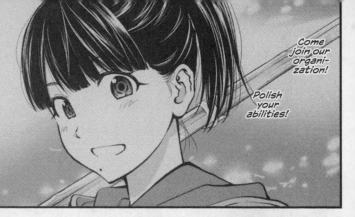

Don't you want to try helping people?

Come join our organiz-ation!

Polish your abilities!

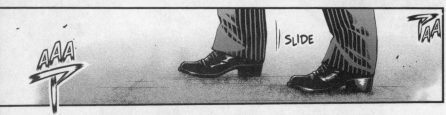

SLIDE

AAA

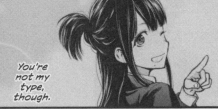

A handsome guy like you probably has girls hanging all over him.

You're not my type, though.

KISS...

ME.

Sorry...

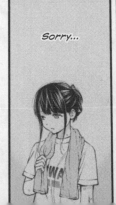

CRUNCH

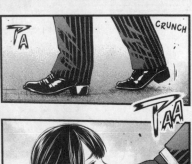

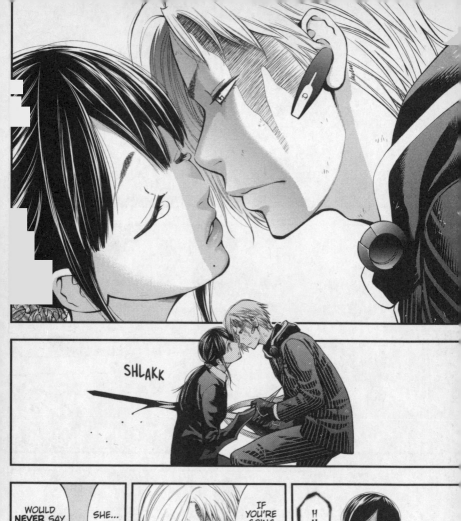

SHLAKK

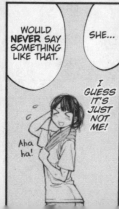

WOULD **NEVER** SAY SOMETHING LIKE THAT.

SHE...

I GUESS IT'S JUST NOT ME!

Aha ha!

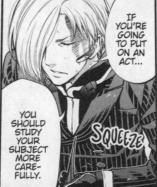

IF YOU'RE GOING TO PUT ON AN ACT...

YOU SHOULD STUDY YOUR SUBJECT MORE CAREFULLY.

SQUEEZE

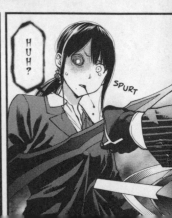

HUH?

SPURT

ESPE-
CIALLY...
NOT...
TO ME.
!!
SHOO
SHOOOM
SLKT
SQUEEZE
HOLD
ON...
MY
BAD...
STOP!
SQUEEZE
SQUEEZE
SQUEEZE
STO--
PWAH!
SPLATTER

I'M OUT OF LTP.
AGH!
TWITCH
YOU WON'T DIE.
GAH...
TWITCH
TWITCH
PA
YOU'RE LUCKY.
PA
PA
SHOO
SHOOOM
I MADE A PROMISE TO MY CHEEKY LITTLE BROTHER.
AUGH!
PA

THEN DIE.
THIS IS IT!
ROKKA! COME!
KAAA
142
You Have Me! ♪
BAM

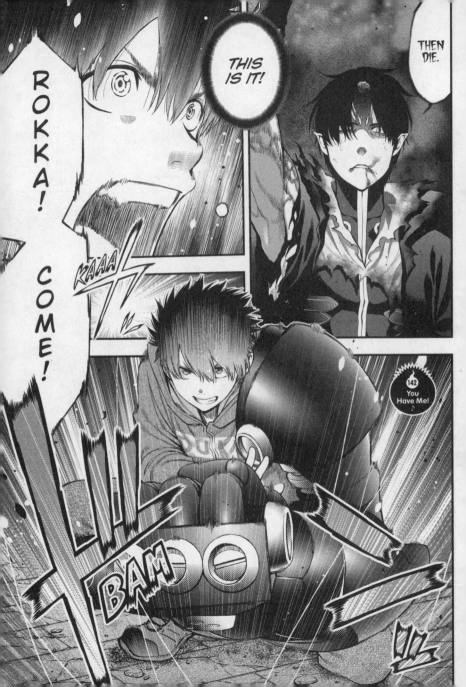

142
You Have Me! ♪

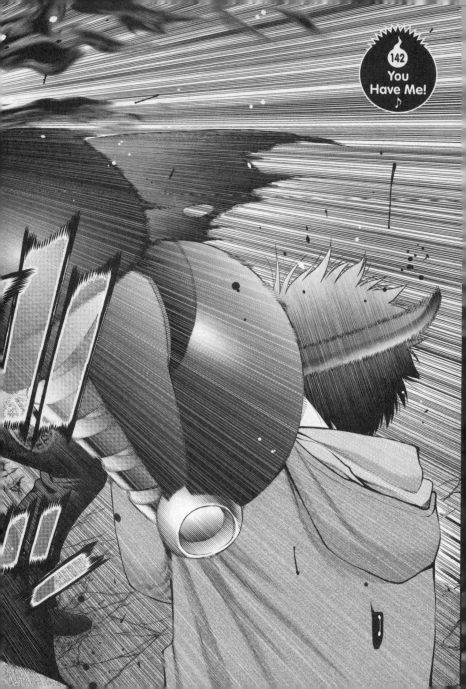

THWACK

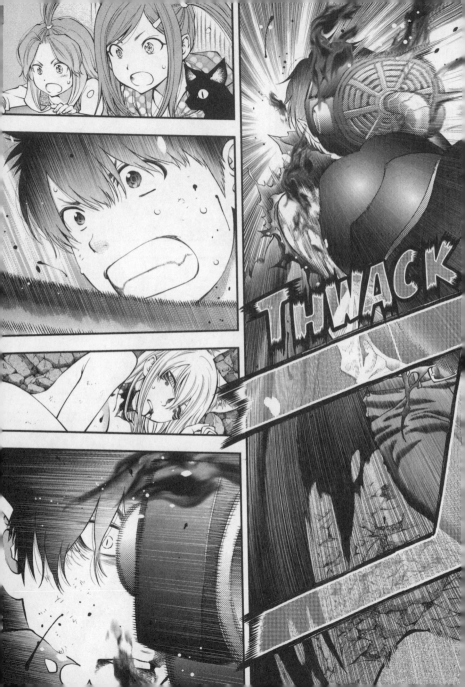

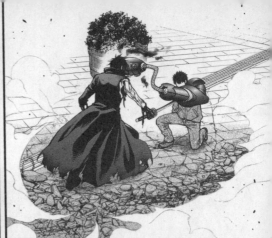

SLIDE

OH!

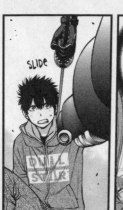

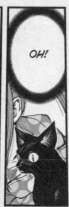

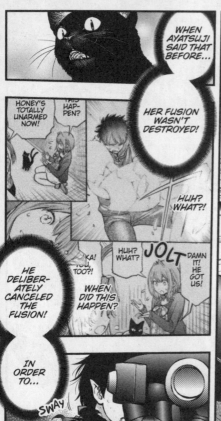

WHEN AYATSUJI SAID THAT BEFORE...

HONEY'S TOTALLY UNARMED NOW!

THIS HAPPEN?

HER FUSION WASN'T DESTROYED!

HUH? WHAT?!

...KA! YOU, TOO?!

HUH? WHAT?

JOLT

DAMN IT! HE GOT US!

WHEN DID THIS HAPPEN?

HE DELIBER-ATELY CANCELED THE FUSION!

IN ORDER TO...

SWAY

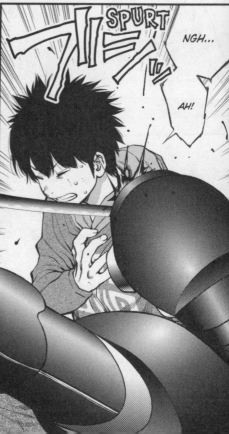

SPURT

NGH...

AH!

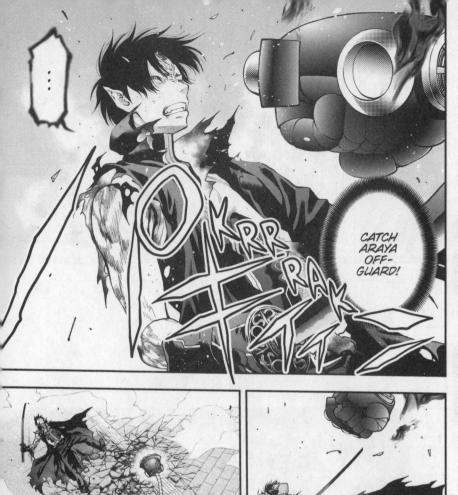

...!

KRR RAK

CATCH ARAYA OFF-GUARD!

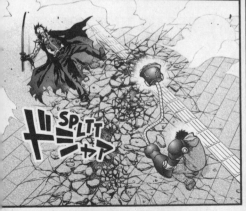

ドSPLTT

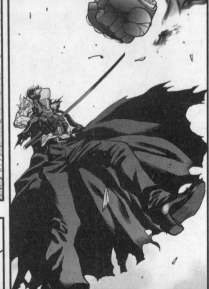

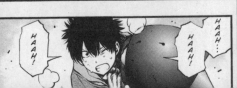

HAAH! HAAH... HAAH!

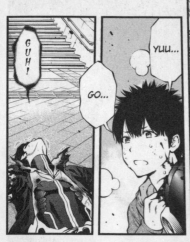

GUH!

YUU...

GO...

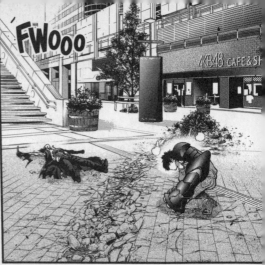

FWOOO

AKB48 CAFE & SI

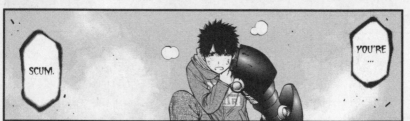

SCUM.

YOU'RE ...

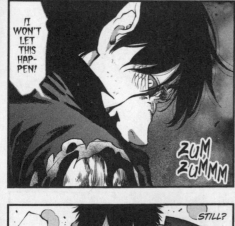

I WON'T LET THIS HAPPEN!

ZUM ZUMMM

YA-TSU...

STILL?

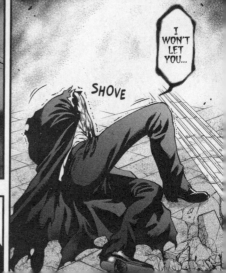

I WON'T LET YOU...

SHOVE

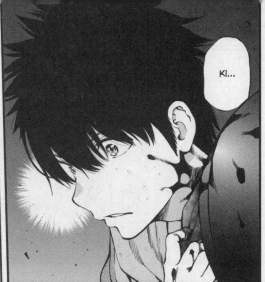

KI...

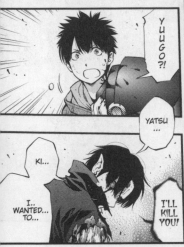

YUUGO?!

YATSU...

KI...

I.. WANTED... TO...

I'LL KILL YOU!

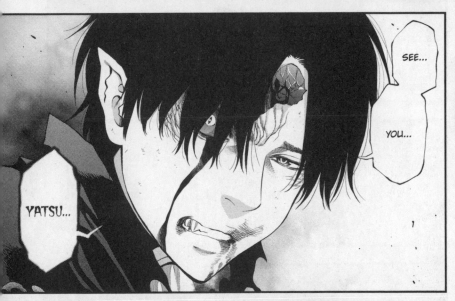

SEE...

YOU...

YATSU...

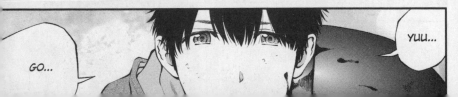

GO...

YUU...

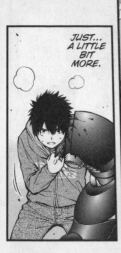

JUST... A LITTLE BIT MORE.

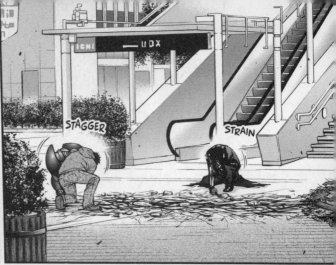

STAGGER

STRAIN

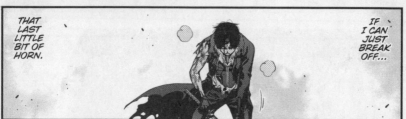

THAT LAST LITTLE BIT OF HORN.

IF I CAN JUST BREAK OFF...

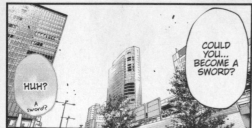

COULD YOU... BECOME A SWORD?

HUH?

A sword?

ROKKA, I'M GONNA ASK SOMETHING CRAZY.

HUH?

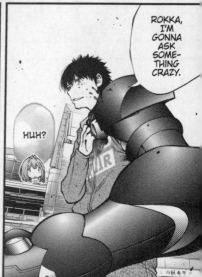

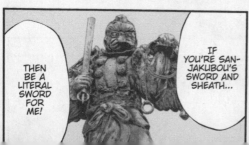

THEN BE A LITERAL SWORD FOR ME!

IF YOU'RE SAN-JAKUBOU'S SWORD AND SHEATH...

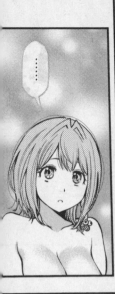

......

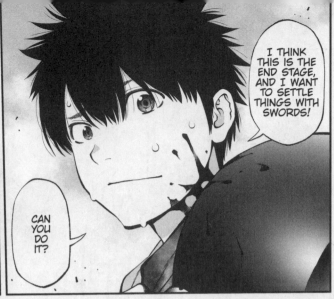

I THINK THIS IS THE END STAGE, AND I WANT TO SETTLE THINGS WITH SWORDS!

CAN YOU DO IT?

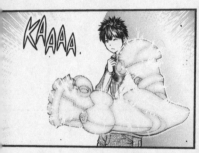

KAAAAA.

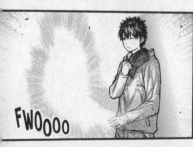

FWOOOO

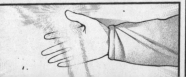

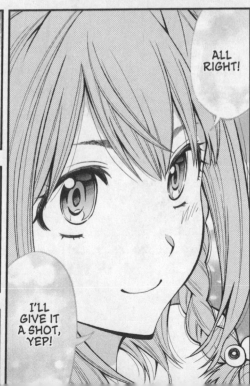

ALL RIGHT!

I'LL GIVE IT A SHOT, YEP!

BAM
SHWOOO
SWING
SO?!
AM I A PROPER SWORD?!
YEAH!
PERFECT! THANKS!

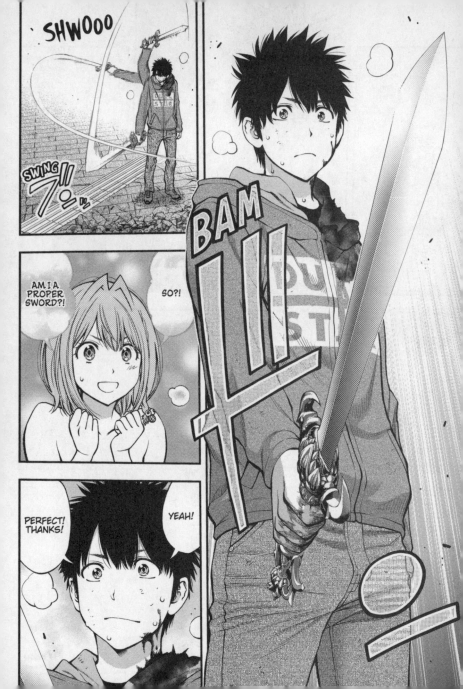

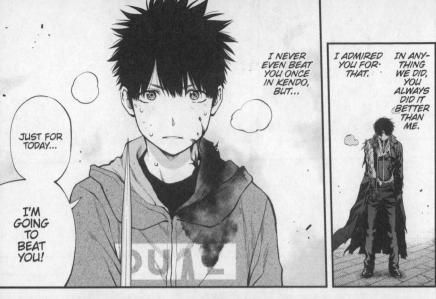

I NEVER EVEN BEAT YOU ONCE IN KENDO, BUT...

JUST FOR TODAY...

I'M GOING TO BEAT YOU!

I ADMIRED YOU FOR THAT.

IN ANYTHING WE DID, YOU ALWAYS DID IT BETTER THAN ME.

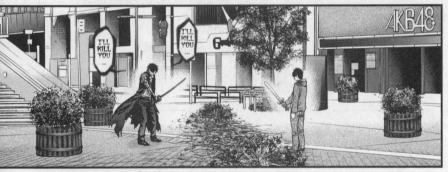

I'LL KILL YOU...

I'LL KILL YOU...

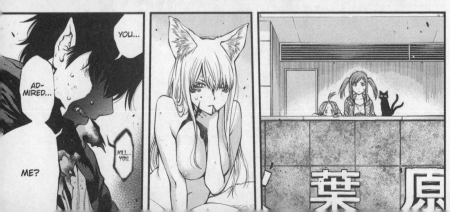

YOU...

AD-MIRED...

ME?

KILL... YOU.

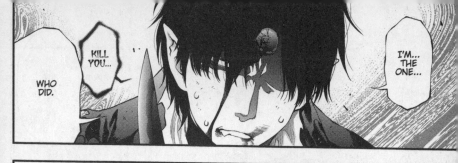

WHO DID.

KILL YOU...

I'M... THE ONE...

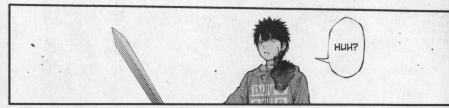

HUH?

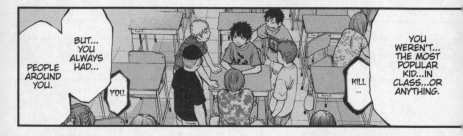

PEOPLE AROUND YOU.

BUT... YOU ALWAYS HAD...

YOU.

YOU WEREN'T... THE MOST POPULAR KID...IN CLASS...OR ANYTHING.

KILL...

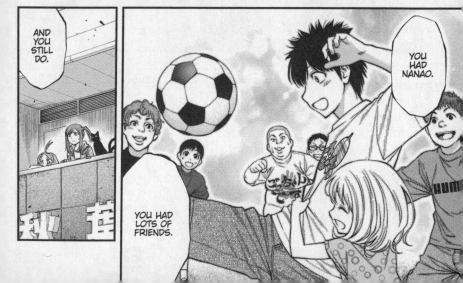

AND YOU STILL DO.

YOU HAD NANAO.

YOU HAD LOTS OF FRIENDS.

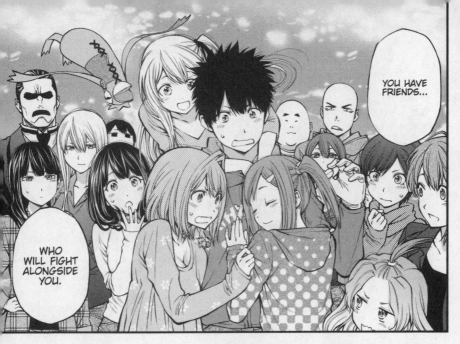

YOU HAVE FRIENDS...

WHO WILL FIGHT ALONGSIDE YOU.

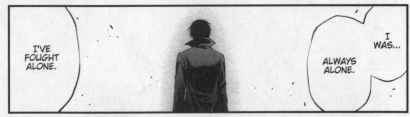

I'VE FOUGHT ALONE.

I WAS...

ALWAYS ALONE.

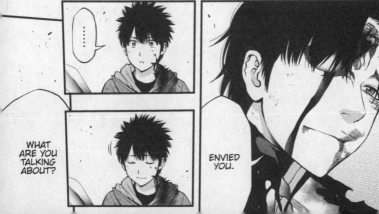

......

WHAT ARE YOU TALKING ABOUT?

I...

ENVIED YOU.

YOU HAVE ME!

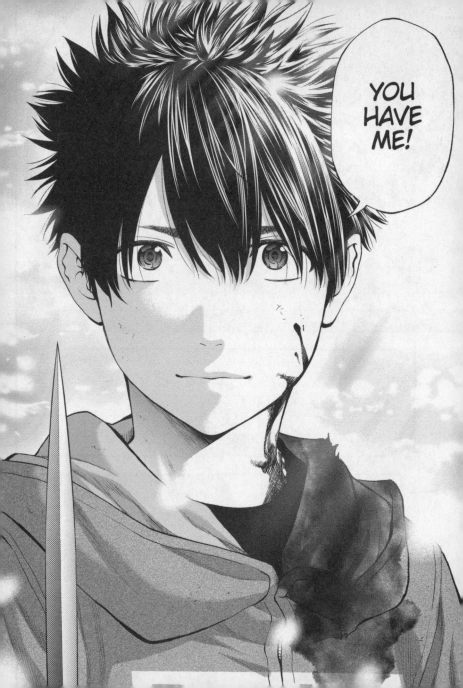

KILL
YOU
...

...

FLASH

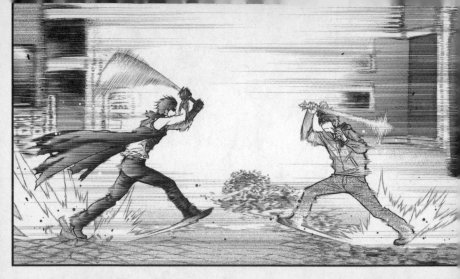

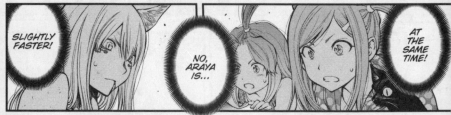

SLIGHTLY FASTER!

NO, ARAYA IS...

AT THE SAME TIME!

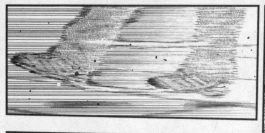

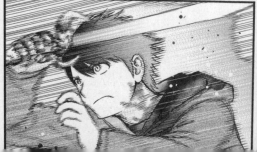

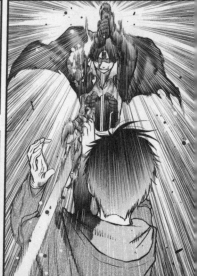

KSHAAAANG

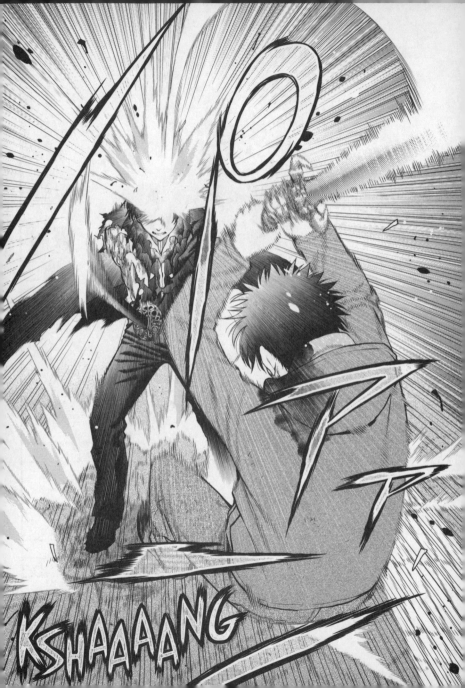

143
Have
I Become
That?

143
Have I Become That? ♪
SPRAAAANG

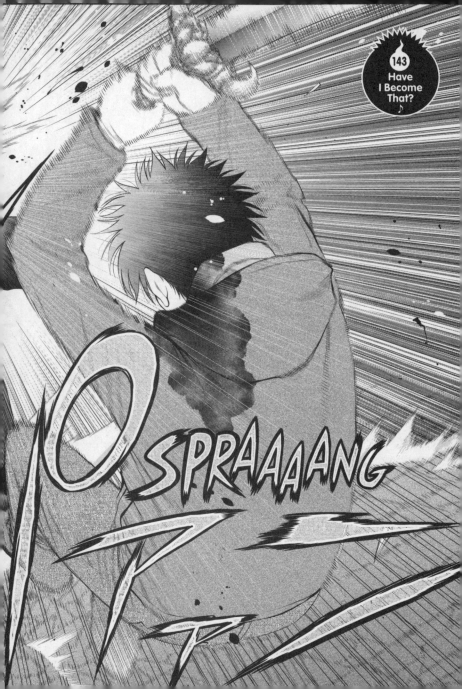

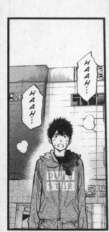

HAAH!..

HAAH!..

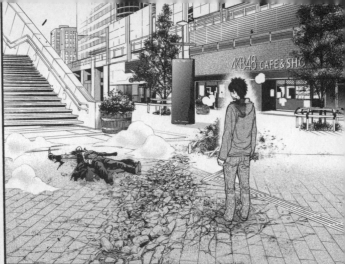

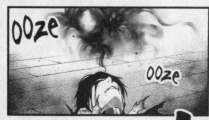

OOZE

OOZE

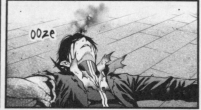

OOZE

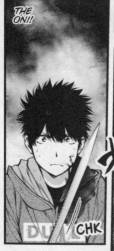

THE ONI!!

CHK

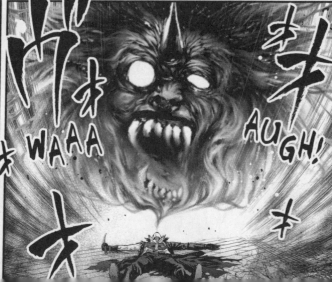

WAAA

AUGH!

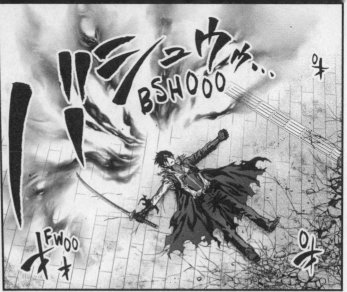

IT... DISAP-PEARED?

BSHOOO

YUU... GO?

FWOO

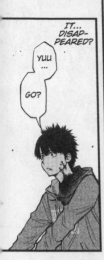

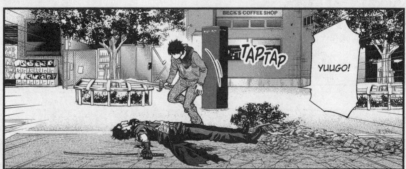

BECK'S COFFEE SHOP

TAP TAP

YUUGO!

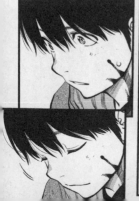

YATSU...

KI...

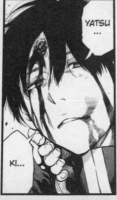

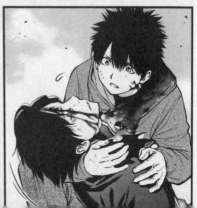

HOW DO YOU LIKE THAT?
MY FIRST VICTORY!
YEAH...!
I LOST!

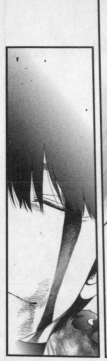

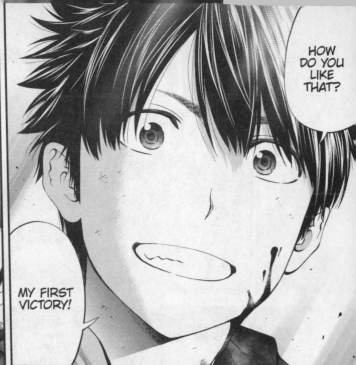

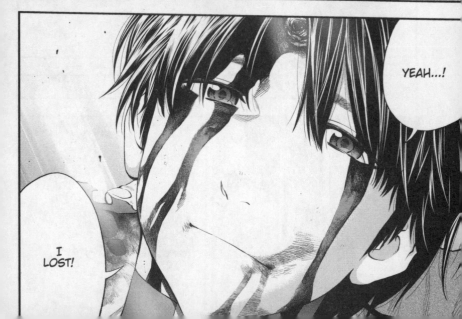

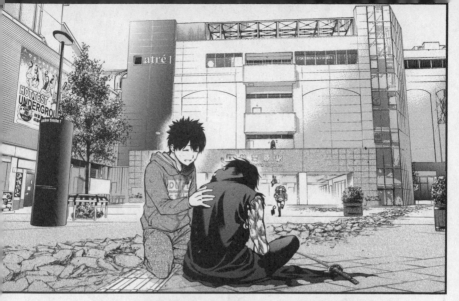

ACK
ACK!

HONEY!

GLOMP

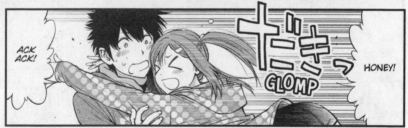

BUT THIS IS ARAYA. I'M SURE THE DAY ISN'T FAR WHEN HE'LL MAKE THAT POWER HIS OWN, JUST AS YATSUKI HAS.

I DOUBT THAT THIS HAS COMPLETELY UNDONE THE CURSE OF KIDOUMARU.

BUT STILL...

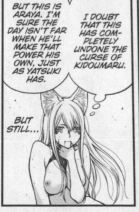

OWWW! I HIT MY BUTT!

WONDER-FUL!

HEY, HEY, HIME-CHAN!

YOU WERE AMAZING, HONEY!

HEY! HIME! WHAT ARE YOU DOING?!

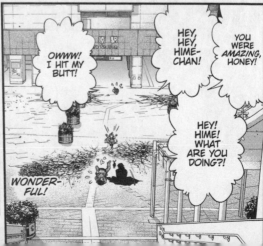

THAT UNRELIABLE BOY...
Ah...!
FLAIL FLAIL FLAIL
SHE HATES MEEEE ......!!!
I'M...
NOT NORMAL, AM I?
YAAGH!!
IT'S A PERVEEERT!!!
!!
HAS COME SUCH A LONG WAY.
My butt hurts!

JANGLE
JANGLE
JANGLE
JANGLE
AWR!
RAA
FWOO
YES!
THUD
THA-

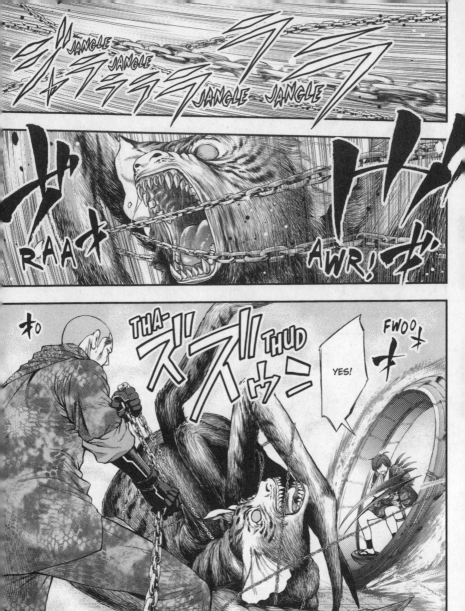

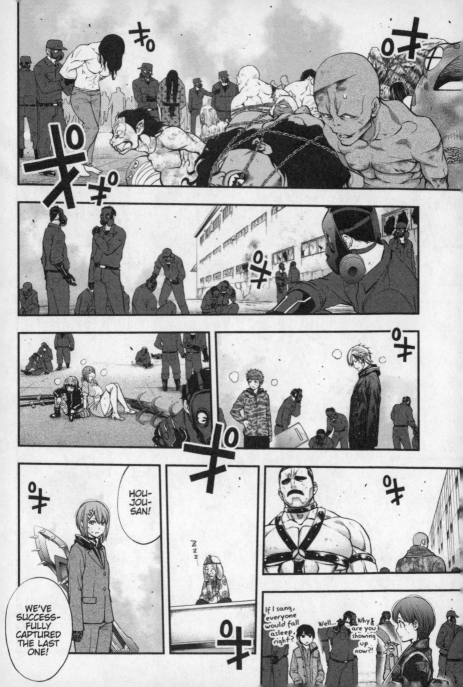

HOU-
JOU-
SAN!

ZZz...

WE'VE
SUCCESS-
FULLY
CAPTURED
THE LAST
ONE!

If I sang,
everyone
would fall
asleep,
right?

Well...

Why
are you
showing
up
now?!

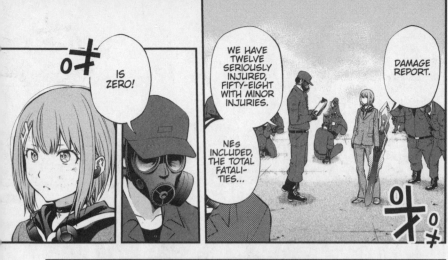

IS ZERO!

WE HAVE TWELVE SERIOUSLY INJURED, FIFTY-EIGHT WITH MINOR INJURIES.

DAMAGE REPORT.

NEs INCLUDED, THE TOTAL FATALI-TIES...

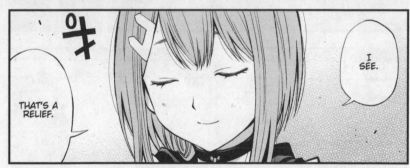

THAT'S A RELIEF.

I SEE.

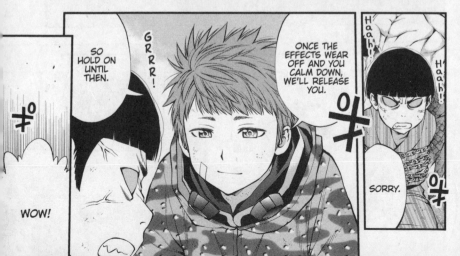

SO HOLD ON UNTIL THEN.

GRRR!

ONCE THE EFFECTS WEAR OFF AND YOU CALM DOWN, WE'LL RELEASE YOU.

Haah!

Haah!

WOW!

SORRY.

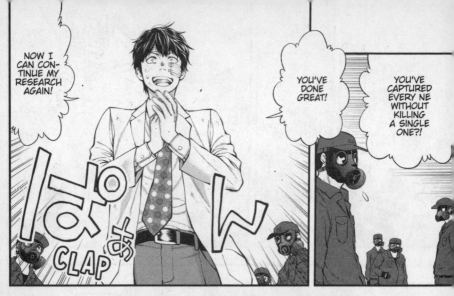

NOW I CAN CON- TINUE MY RESEARCH AGAIN!

YOU'VE DONE GREAT!

YOU'VE CAPTURED EVERY NE WITHOUT KILLING A SINGLE ONE?!

ﾊｯ ﾊｯ

CLAP

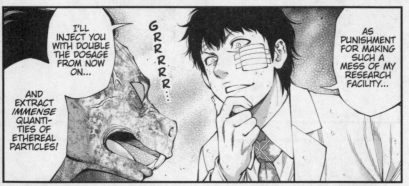

I'LL INJECT YOU WITH DOUBLE THE DOSAGE FROM NOW ON...

GRRRR...

AND EXTRACT *IMMENSE* QUANTI- TIES OF ETHEREAL PARTICLES!

AS PUNISHMENT FOR MAKING SUCH A MESS OF MY RESEARCH FACILITY...

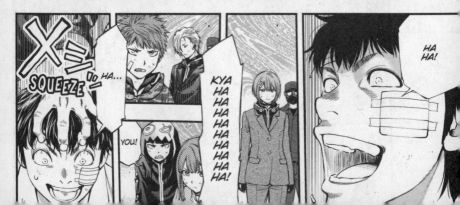

ﾒﾐ

SQUEEZE

HA...

KYA HA HA HA HA HA HA HA!

YOU!

HA HA!

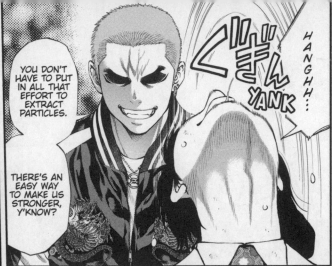

WH-WHO THE HELL ARE YOU?! LET ME GO!

YOU DON'T HAVE TO PUT IN ALL THAT EFFORT TO EXTRACT PARTICLES.

HANGHH...

YANK

THERE'S AN EASY WAY TO MAKE US STRONGER, Y'KNOW?

YOU DO IT...

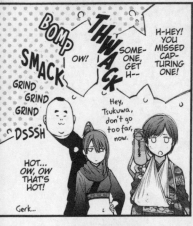

BOMP

OW!

THWACK

SOMEONE, GET H--

H-HEY! YOU MISSED CAPTURING ONE!

SMACK

GRIND GRIND GRIND

DSSSH

Hey, Tsukuwa, don't go too far, now.

HOT... OW, OW THAT'S HOT!

Gerk...

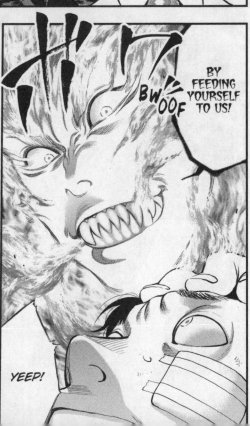

BWOOF

BY FEEDING YOURSELF TO US!

YIKES.

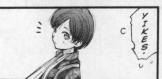

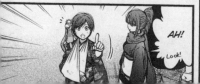

AH! Look!

YEEP!

JUNK SHOP
CAN I...

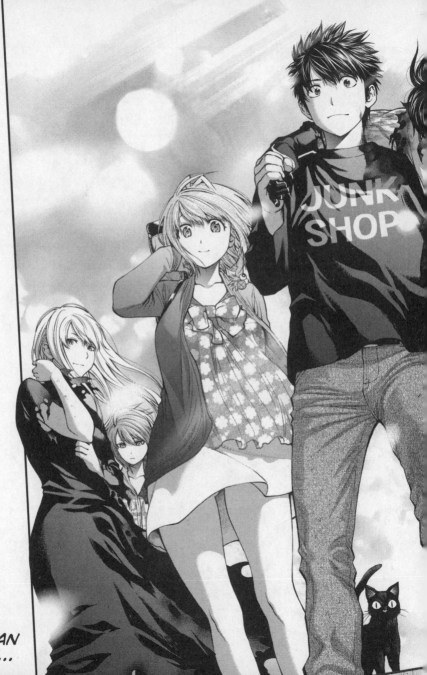

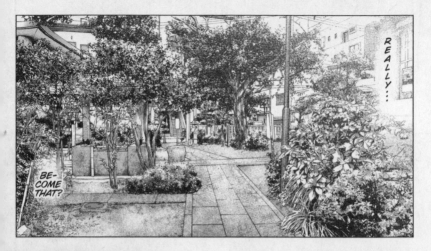

REALLY...

BE-
COME
THAT?

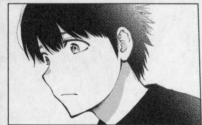

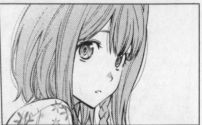

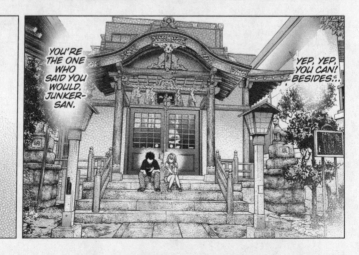

YOU'RE THE ONE WHO SAID YOU WOULD, JUNKER-SAN.

YEP, YEP, YOU CAN! BESIDES...

YEAH.

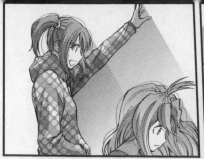
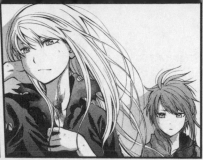

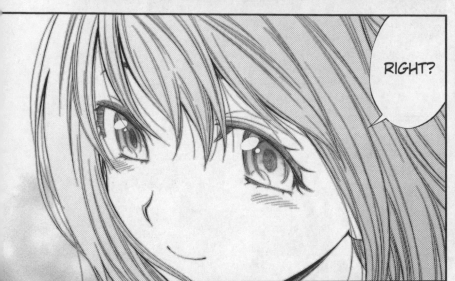

RIGHT?

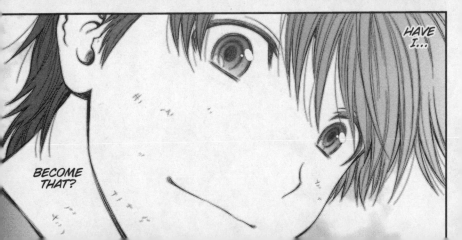

HAVE I...

BECOME THAT?

A BRIDGE...
CONNECTING HUMANS AND YOKAI?
YEAH!

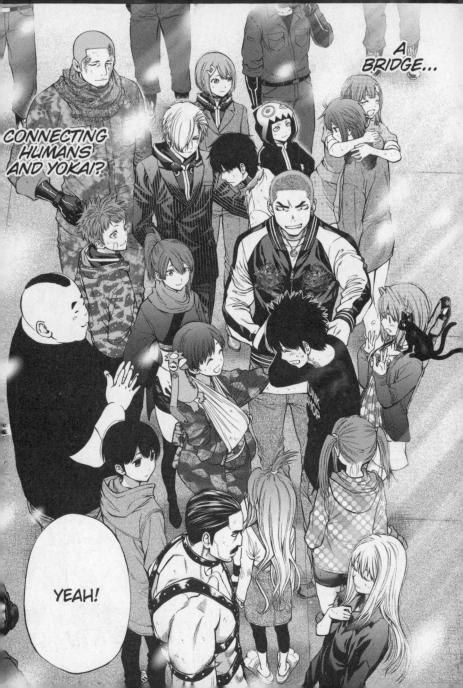

144
Let's Be Good
Friends! ♪

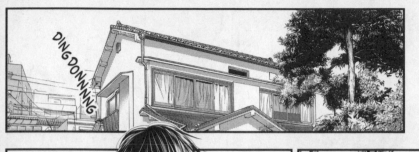

DING DONNNG

HELLO.

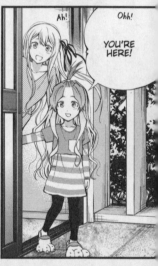

Ah!

Ohh!

YOU'RE HERE!

Hey, Nana—chan.

It's Yuugo—kun!

IT'S RATHER BOISTER-OUS IN THERE RIGHT NOW, BUT...WELL, COME IN!

THANK YOU.

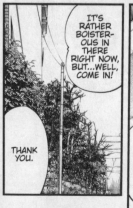

YEAH, I WASN'T TOO BANGED UP.

HERE, FOR EVERY-ONE.

OH! YOU DIDN'T HAVE TO.

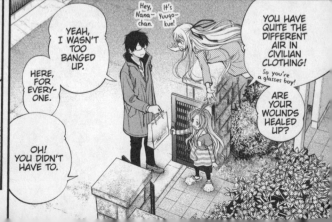

YOU HAVE QUITE THE DIFFERENT AIR IN CIVILIAN CLOTHING!

So you're a glasses boy!

ARE YOUR WOUNDS HEALED UP?

HERE! SAY AHH, JUNKER-SAN! ♡
MINE'S BETTER THAN ROKKA'S!
SAY AHH! ♡
I-IF YOU LIKE, YOU COULD TRY MINE, TOO.
Ah, um...
S--
SAY, AHH...
Ha ha... ha...
Even Moru-chan!
THEY'RE THE SAME THING! THERE'S NO WAY YOURS COULD TASTE BETTER, HIME-CHAN!
BICKER BICKER
AND HEY, WHY ARE YOU NONCHALANTLY JOINING IN ON THIS?!
HUH?! I, UM...
Why am I?
You can do it, Momo!
SHUT UP! THERE'S A DIFFERENCE IN LOVE! LOVE!
(Kirue)
MINE HAS A SUPER-SIZED SERVING OF LOVE!
(Rokka)
You're not joining in?
What?! Why would I?!
SHUT UP! CAIN'T YA EAT IN SILENCE?!
HERE, YATSUKI-SAMA! SAY AHH! ♡
SHOVE
AHHHHHH!

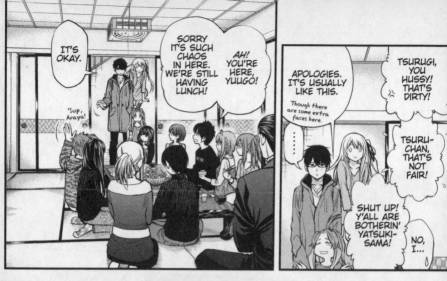

IT'S OKAY.

SORRY IT'S SUCH CHAOS IN HERE. WE'RE STILL HAVING LUNCH!

AH! YOU'RE HERE, YUUGO!

'Sup, Araya!

APOLOGIES. IT'S USUALLY LIKE THIS.

Though there are some extra faces here.

......

TSURUGI, YOU HUSSY! THAT'S DIRTY!

TSURU-CHAN, THAT'S NOT FAIR!

SHUT UP! Y'ALL ARE BOTHERIN' YATSUKI-SAMA!

NO, I...

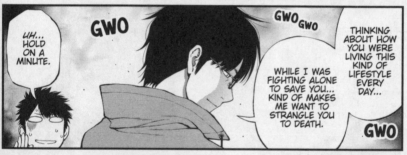

UH... HOLD ON A MINUTE.

GWO GWO GWO

WHILE I WAS FIGHTING ALONE TO SAVE YOU... KIND OF MAKES ME WANT TO STRANGLE YOU TO DEATH.

THINKING ABOUT HOW YOU WERE LIVING THIS KIND OF LIFESTYLE EVERY DAY...

GWO

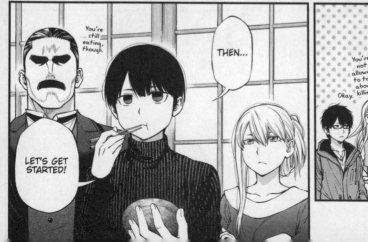

You're still eating, though.

THEN...

LET'S GET STARTED!

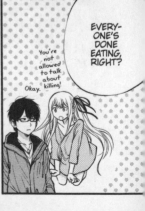

EVERYONE'S DONE EATING, RIGHT?

You're not allowed to talk about killing!

Okay.

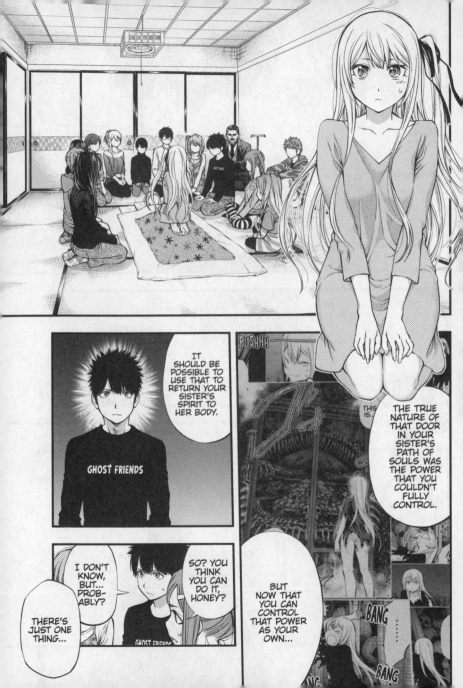

IT SHOULD BE POSSIBLE TO USE THAT TO RETURN YOUR SISTER'S SPIRIT TO HER BODY.

GHOST FRIENDS

PUSHHH

THIS IS...

THE TRUE NATURE OF THAT DOOR IN YOUR SISTER'S PATH OF SOULS WAS THE POWER THAT YOU COULDN'T FULLY CONTROL.

I DON'T KNOW, BUT... PROB-ABLY?

SO? YOU THINK YOU CAN DO IT, HONEY?

THERE'S JUST ONE THING...

BUT NOW THAT YOU CAN CONTROL THAT POWER AS YOUR OWN...

GHOST FRIENDS

BANG

BANG

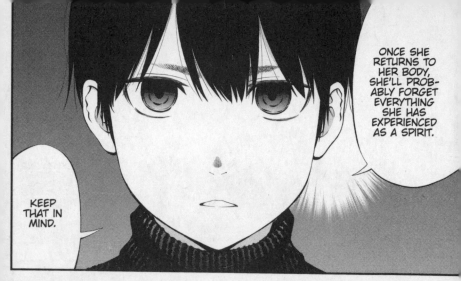

ONCE SHE RETURNS TO HER BODY, SHE'LL PROBABLY FORGET EVERYTHING SHE HAS EXPERIENCED AS A SPIRIT.

KEEP THAT IN MIND.

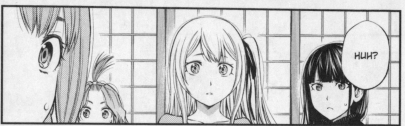

HUH?

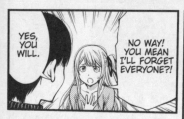

YES, YOU WILL.

NO WAY! YOU MEAN I'LL FORGET EVERYONE?!

THEY FORM AN UNCONSCIOUS BELIEF THAT THEIR EXPERIENCES WERE A DREAM, AND FORGET IT ALL.

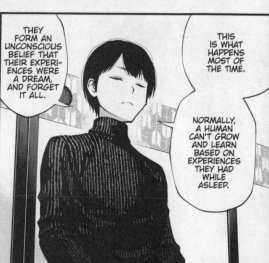

THIS IS WHAT HAPPENS MOST OF THE TIME.

NORMALLY, A HUMAN CAN'T GROW AND LEARN BASED ON EXPERIENCES THEY HAD WHILE ASLEEP.

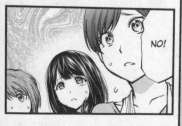

NO!

NANAO DOESN'T WANT THAT!
EVEN FIGHTING WITH EVERYONE. NO WAY!
FORGETTING MEETING EVERYONE, AND PLAYING WITH EVERY-ONE...
NO WAY NO WAY!
ばっ
SWOOP
NANAO!
NANA-CHAN!

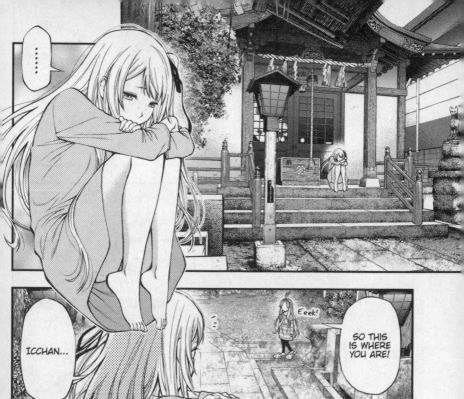

.....

ICCHAN...

Eeek!

SO THIS
IS WHERE
YOU ARE!

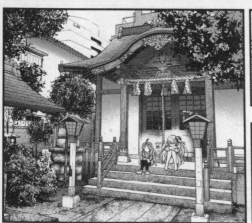

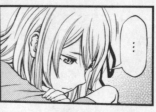

...

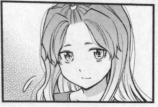

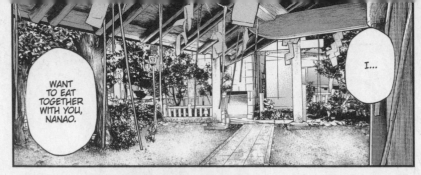

I...

WANT TO EAT TOGETHER WITH YOU, NANAO.

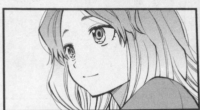
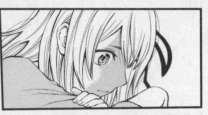

HUH?

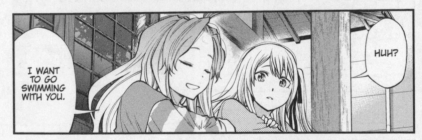

I WANT TO GO SWIMMING WITH YOU.

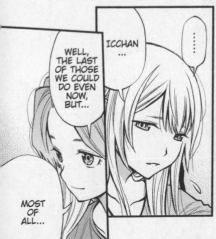

ICCHAN...

......

WELL, THE LAST OF THOSE WE COULD DO EVEN NOW, BUT...

MOST OF ALL...

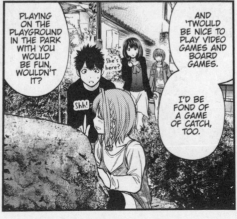

PLAYING ON THE PLAYGROUND IN THE PARK WITH YOU WOULD BE FUN, WOULDN'T IT?

AND 'TWOULD BE NICE TO PLAY VIDEO GAMES AND BOARD GAMES.

I'D BE FOND OF A GAME OF CATCH, TOO.

She's here?

Shh!

I WANT TO MEET YOU IN THE FLESH!
IT'S ALL RIGHT.
WE'LL MEET AGAIN.
MAKE FRIENDS ALL OVER AGAIN.
HAVE FUN AGAIN!
DOUBLE THE FUN, IN A WAY!

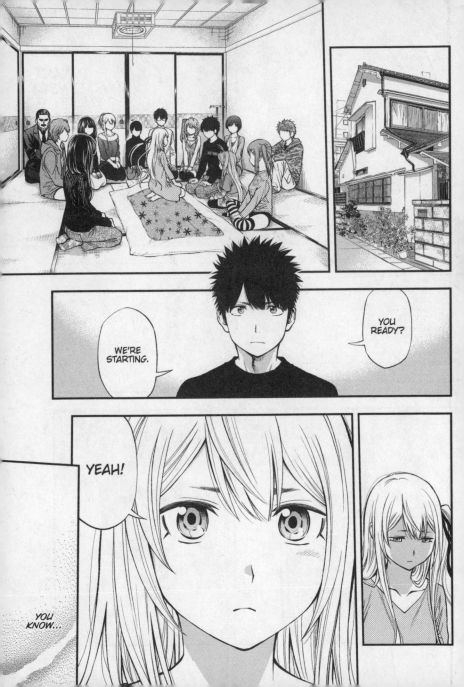

YOU
READY?

WE'RE
STARTING.

YEAH!

YOU
KNOW...

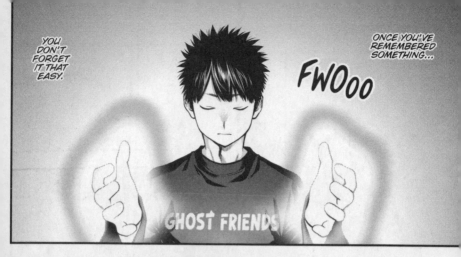

ONCE YOU'VE REMEMBERED SOMETHING...

YOU DON'T FORGET IT THAT EASY.

FWOoo

GHOST FRIENDS

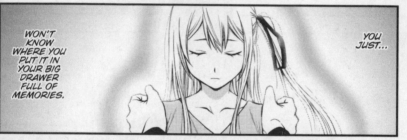

YOU JUST...

WON'T KNOW WHERE YOU PUT IT IN YOUR BIG DRAWER FULL OF MEMORIES.

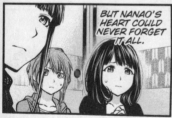

BUT NANAO'S HEART COULD NEVER FORGET IT ALL.

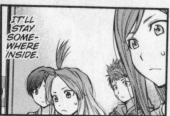

IT'LL STAY SOME-WHERE INSIDE.

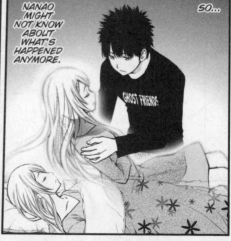

NANAO MIGHT NOT KNOW ABOUT WHAT'S HAPPENED ANYMORE.

SO...

IT'LL STAY FOR-EVER AND EVER...
DEEP, DEEP INSIDE NANAO'S HEART.
SO...
EVEN IF IT FEELS LIKE OUR FIRST TIME MEETING EACH OTHER...
LET'S PLAY...
LIKE WE'RE PICKING UP RIGHT WHERE WE LEFT OFF TODAY!

NANAO?

NANAO!

BLINK

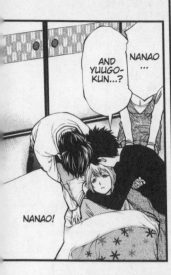

AND YUUGO-KUN...?

NANAO...

NANAO!

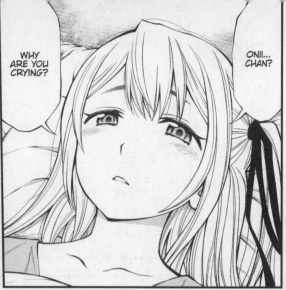

WHY ARE YOU CRYING?

ONII... CHAN?

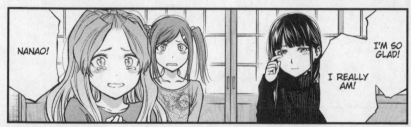

NANAO!

I'M SO GLAD! I REALLY AM!

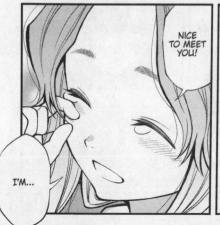

NICE TO MEET YOU!

I'M...

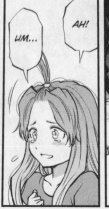

UM...

AH!

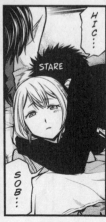

HIC...

STARE

SOB...

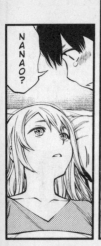

NANAO?

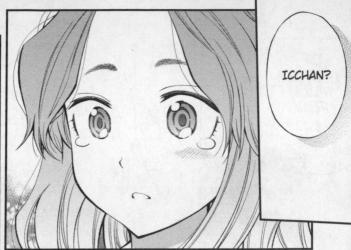

ICCHAN?

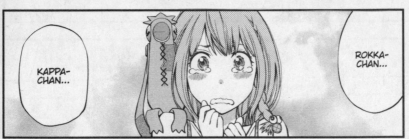

KAPPA-CHAN...

ROKKA-CHAN...

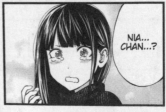

NIA-CHAN...?

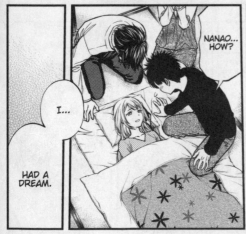

NANAO... HOW?

I...

HAD A DREAM.

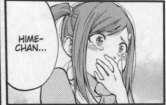

HIME-CHAN...

I DREAMT I WAS PLAYING WITH YOU ALL!
IT WAS SO MUCH FUN!

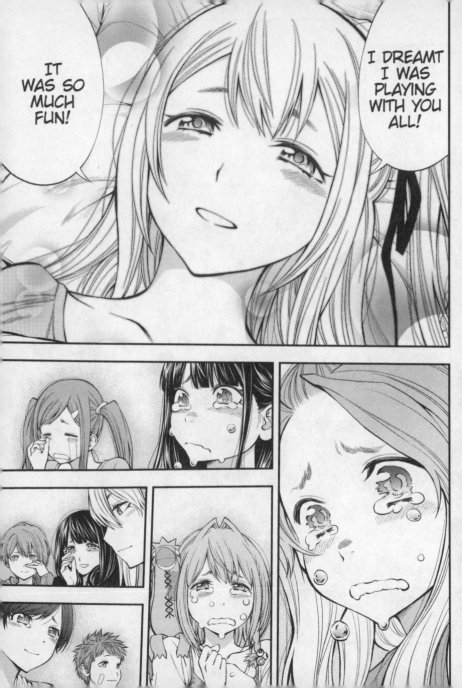

HI, I'M NANAO. NICE TO MEET YOU!
LET'S KEEP ON...
BEING GOOD FRIENDS!

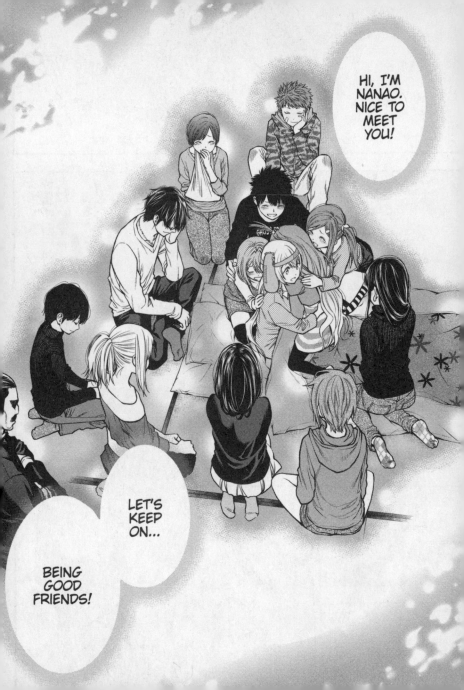

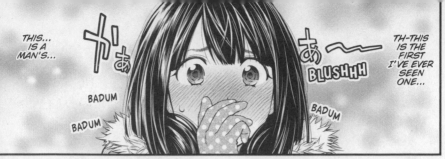

THIS... IS A MAN'S...

BADUM

BADUM

BLUSHHH

TH-THIS IS THE FIRST I'VE EVER SEEN ONE...

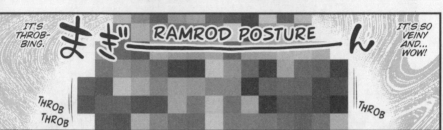

IT'S THROB-BING.

RAMROD POSTURE

IT'S SO VEINY AND... WOW!

THROB THROB

THROB

145

I'm Gonna Change!! ♪

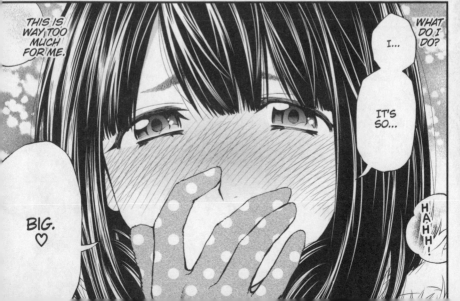

THIS IS WAY TOO MUCH FOR ME.

I...

IT'S SO...

WHAT DO I DO?

HAHH!

BIG. ♡

TOIPO... HUH? WHAT?
A TOIPOKUN-OYASHI!
IT'S A YOKAI FROM THE AINU REGIONS.
IT SEEMS ONE HAS BEEN APPEARING AROUND HERE RECENTLY, AND IT'S BEEN CAUSING QUITE A LOT OF MAY-HEM.
IT ONLY TARGETS WOMEN, SO WE CAN ASSUME IT'S MALE, BUT...
IT'S AN EXTREMELY RARE TYPE OF YOKAI. IF POSSIBLE, I'D LIKE YOU TO CAPTURE IT.
ROGER!
BY THE WAY, NAGI-SAN...
CAN I ASK SOME-THING?
HMM?

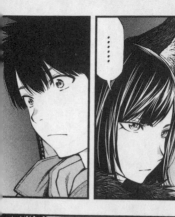

ABOUT...

MORU-CHAN.

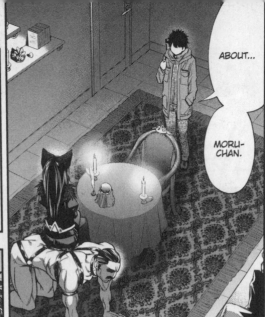

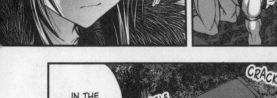

A LONG TIME AGO...

IN THE MIDDLE OF THE WILDERNESS SOMEWHERE, A CAR WAS ATTACKED BY A NOZUCHI.

GURGLE GURGLE

CRACK

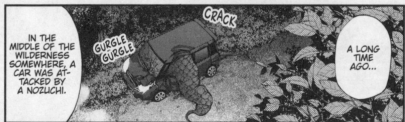

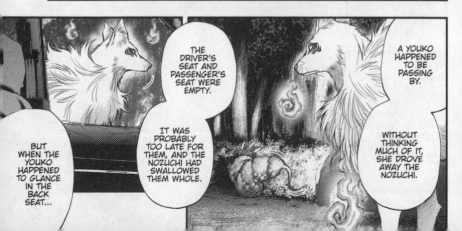

A YOUKO HAPPENED TO BE PASSING BY.

WITHOUT THINKING MUCH OF IT, SHE DROVE AWAY THE NOZUCHI.

THE DRIVER'S SEAT AND PASSENGER'S SEAT WERE EMPTY.

IT WAS PROBABLY TOO LATE FOR THEM, AND THE NOZUCHI HAD SWALLOWED THEM WHOLE.

BUT WHEN THE YOUKO HAPPENED TO GLANCE IN THE BACK SEAT...

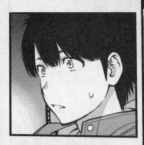

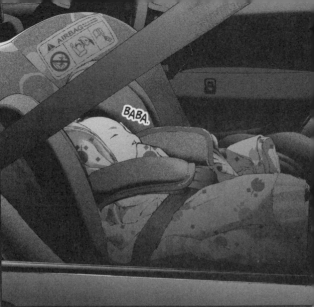

BABA.

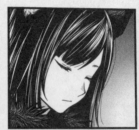

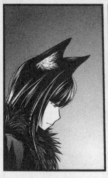

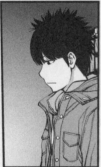

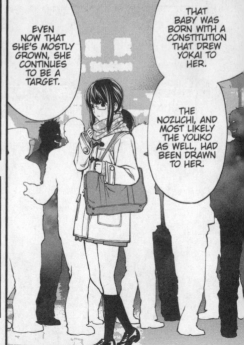

EVEN NOW THAT SHE'S MOSTLY GROWN, SHE CONTINUES TO BE A TARGET.

THAT BABY WAS BORN WITH A CONSTITUTION THAT DREW YOKAI TO HER.

THE NOZUCHI, AND MOST LIKELY THE YOUKO AS WELL, HAD BEEN DRAWN TO HER.

COULD YOU...

CONTINUE TO KEEP HER SAFE?

OF COURSE!
THANK YOU.
Open

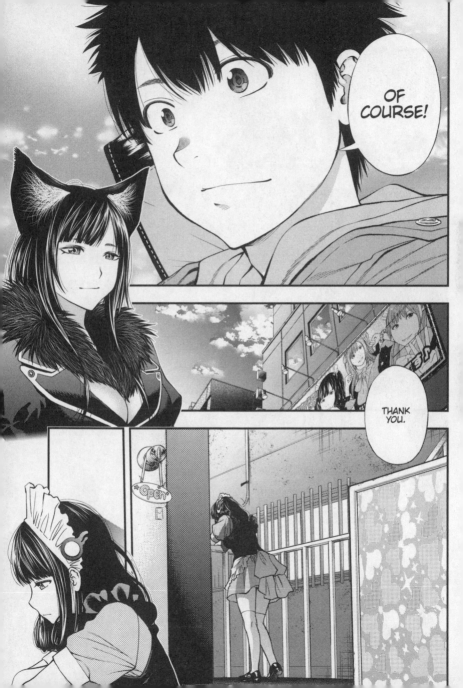

IN FRONT OF THE GIRL I LOVE, AT LEAST!
......
NO.
IT'S NOT ABOUT WHO YAKKI-SAN LIKES.
THE QUESTION IS: WHAT DO I WANT TO DO?
I'M NOT GONNA LET YOU...
I...
YOU TOO, MORU-CHAN!
SO HIGH UP, SO I THOUGHT MAYBE YOU'D DIED!
DON'T YOU WORRY ABOUT IT
CRAACK

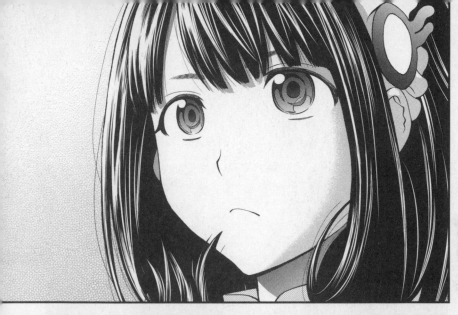

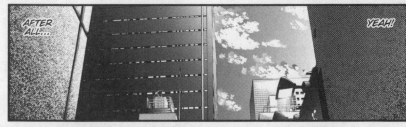

AFTER ALL...

YEAH!

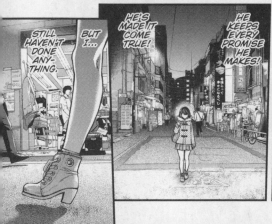

STILL HAVEN'T DONE ANY-THING.

BUT I...

HE'S MADE IT COME TRUE!

HE KEEPS EVERY PROMISE HE MAKES!

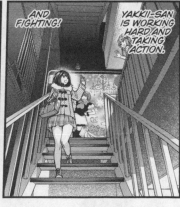

AND FIGHTING!

YAKKII-SAN IS WORKING HARD AND TAKING ACTION.

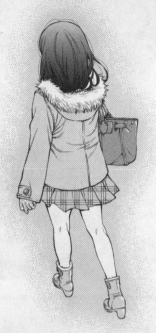

I LOVE
HIM.

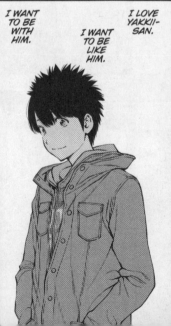

I WANT
TO BE
WITH
HIM.

I WANT
TO BE
LIKE
HIM.

I LOVE
YAKKII-
SAN.

I CAN'T
JUST WAIT
AROUND!

I HAVE TO
CHANGE...

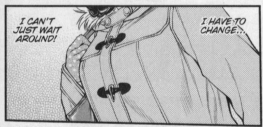

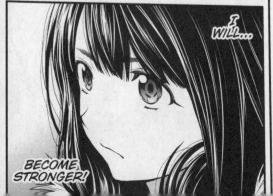

I
WILL...

BECOME
STRONGER!

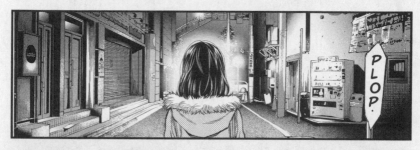

PLOP.

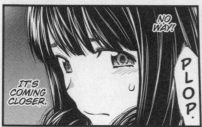

NO WAY!

IT'S COMING CLOSER.

PLOP.

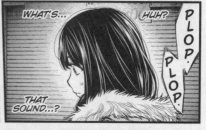

WHAT'S...

HUH?

PLOP.

PLOP.

THAT SOUND...?

BY THE WAY, NAGI-SAN, THAT THING...

WHAT SORT OF YOKAI IS IT?

THE TOIPOKUN-OYASHI?

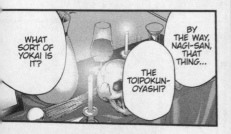

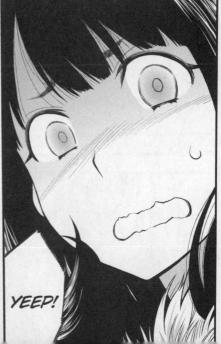

HEH.

LIKE?

IT LOOKS LIKE...

I TOLD YOU IT WAS RARE, RIGHT?

JUST LIKE IT.

YEAH.

JUST LIKE IT?

It, what's "it?"

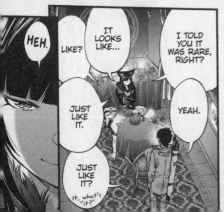

YEEP!

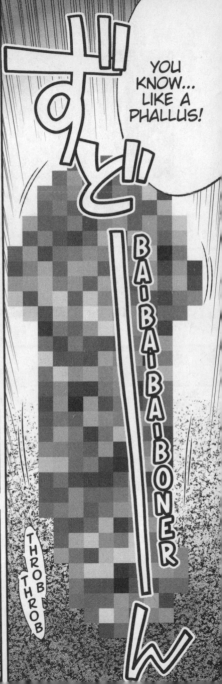

WHAT IS THIS?! WHAT IS THIS?! WHAT IS THIS THING?!

A DI... GROWING FROM THE GROUND!!

HGYAAAAAH!

YOU KNOW... LIKE A PHALLUS!

TOIPOKUN-OYASHI

A yokai told of by the Karafuto Ainu.

It's unknown whether they lurk underground and only show that part above ground, or if that part is their full body, but it's said that when a woman is walking out in the forests or fields, suddenly a mushroom-like thing will appear in her path and bobble toward her.

It's unusual for a yokai to be only genitals like this, and no other examples can be seen in Japan.

BYOING

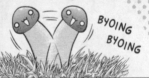

BYOING BYOING

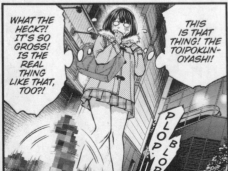

WHAT THE HECK?! IT'S SO GROSS! IS THE REAL THING LIKE THAT, TOO?!

THIS IS THAT THING! THE TOIPOKUN-OYASHI!!

PLOP PLOP PLOP

WAIT, THIS ISN'T THE TIME TO BE THINKING STUFF LIKE THAT!
I HAVE TO RUN!
DASH
YEEK!
ZOOM
PLOP
BOING BOING
NOO...
くるっ
WHIRL
ZOOM
PLOP
HYAAAAH!!
NO WAY!
HOW CAN IT BE SO FAST WHEN IT'S SHAPED LIKE THAT?!
I CAN'T GET AWAY?!
When you encounter a toipokun-oyashi...
there's an easy way to make it run away.
AH!
Oh, yeah! I remember, she said...
First, you compliment it!
RIGHT!
FIRST, I COMPLIMENT IT!

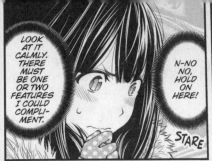

LOOK AT IT CALMLY. THERE MUST BE ONE OR TWO FEATURES I COULD COMPLIMENT.

N-NO NO, HOLD ON HERE!

STARE

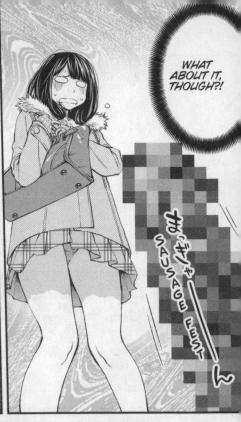

WHAT ABOUT IT, THOUGH?!

SAUSAGE FEST

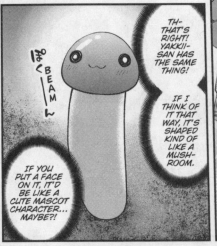

BEAM

TH-THAT'S RIGHT! YAKKII-SAN HAS THE SAME THING!

IF I THINK OF IT THAT WAY, IT'S SHAPED KIND OF LIKE A MUSH-ROOM.

IF YOU PUT A FACE ON IT, IT'D BE LIKE A CUTE MASCOT CHARACTER... MAYBE?!

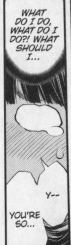

WHAT DO I DO, WHAT DO I DO?! WHAT SHOULD I...

Y-- YOU'RE SO...

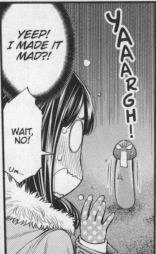

YEEP! I MADE IT MAD?!

YAAARGH!

WAIT, NO!

Um...

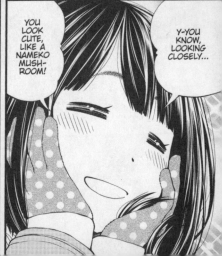

YOU LOOK CUTE, LIKE A NAMEKO MUSH-ROOM!

Y-YOU KNOW, LOOKING CLOSELY...

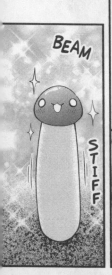

BEAM

STIFF

I'VE NEVER SEEN ONE SO BIG. ♡

B-BIG!

HAHH!

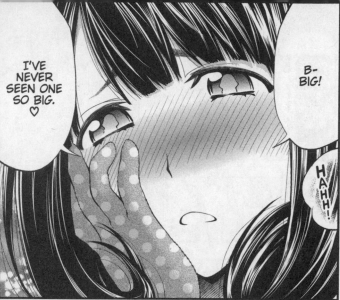

"Would you like to go a round?"

"But I'm just as good, you know?"

Then it will leave in satis-faction, so they say.

THRUST THRUST THRUST

I...

SO, NEXT IS...

Yeah! So big! And hard! Amazing! Right right?!

Right?!

GOOD, GOOD!

THIS IS LOOKING PRETTY GOOD!

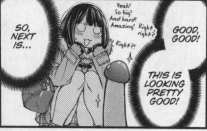

And while showing it, your lower body, rock your hips as if you're having sex and say this!

Next, you take off your under-wear.

UNDER ...?

SE...

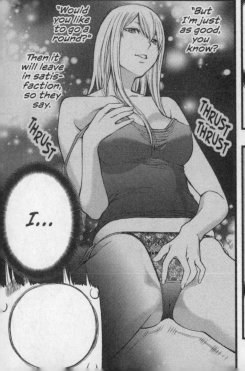

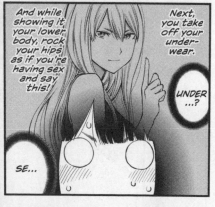

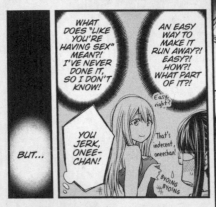

WHAT DOES "LIKE YOU'RE HAVING SEX" MEAN?! I'VE NEVER DONE IT, SO I DON'T KNOW!

AN EASY WAY TO MAKE IT RUN AWAY?! EASY?! HOW?! WHAT PART OF IT?!

BUT...

Easy, right?

YOU JERK, ONEE-CHAN!

That's indecent, oneechan!

BYOING BYOING

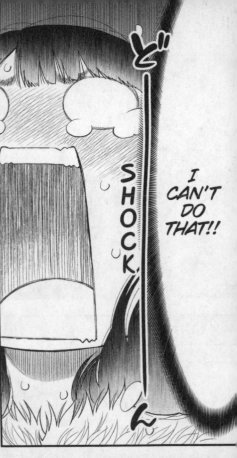

I CAN'T DO THAT!!

SHOCK.

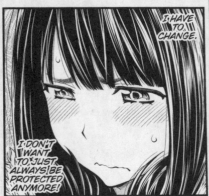

I HAVE TO... CHANGE.

I DON'T WANT TO JUST ALWAYS BE PROTECTED ANYMORE!

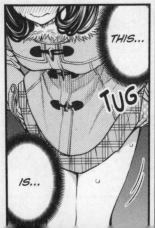

THIS...

TUG

IS...

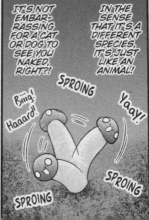

IT'S NOT EMBAR-RASSING FOR A CAT OR DOG TO SEE YOU NAKED, RIGHT?!

IN THE SENSE THAT IT'S A DIFFERENT SPECIES, IT'S JUST LIKE AN ANIMAL!

SPROING

Biiig! Haaard!

Yaay!

SPROING

SPROING

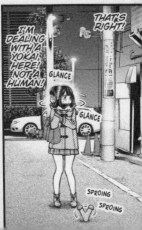

I'M DEALING WITH A YOKAI HERE! NOT A HUMAN!

THAT'S RIGHT!

GLANCE

GLANCE

SPROING

SPROING

ずぼーっ
YANK
NOT EMBARRASSING!
I...
I...
I... CAN...
SQUEEZE
I CAN CHANGE!
DASH
MORU-CHAN!
I WON'T BACK DOWN!

IF YOU WANT...
YANK
WE COULD DO IT?!

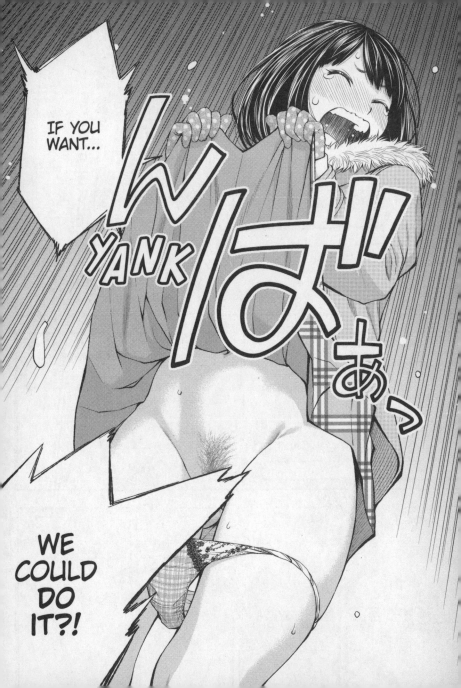

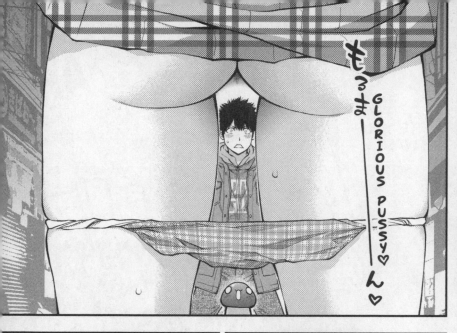

GLORIOUS PUSSY♡

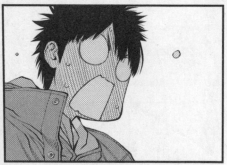

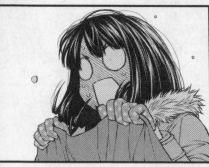

AH!
HEY...

DASH

WAHHHH!

SHOVE

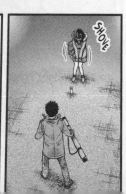

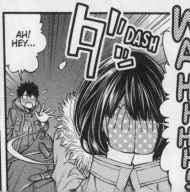

!

TUG

TRIP

ZPLAT

MORU...

YEEK!

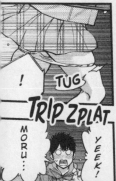

AH.
FULL MOON
SPURT
M-NO MOOOOOORE!
I'LL KILL YOU AND THEN MYSELF, YAKKII-SAN!
I-I DIDN'T SEE ANYTHING! IT WAS TOO DARK FOR ME TO SEE ANYTHING!!
IT'S DARK?!
NO! I DON'T MEAN YOUR-- THAT WASN'T DARK AT ALL!
SO YOU *DID* SEE IT, AFTER ALL!
NO, UM...
WAHHHHH!
YOU'RE GOING TO TAKE RESPON-SIBILITY FOR THIS!
HUH?! RESPON-SIBILITY?!
SATISFIEEED
FIGURE THAT OUT YOURSELF!

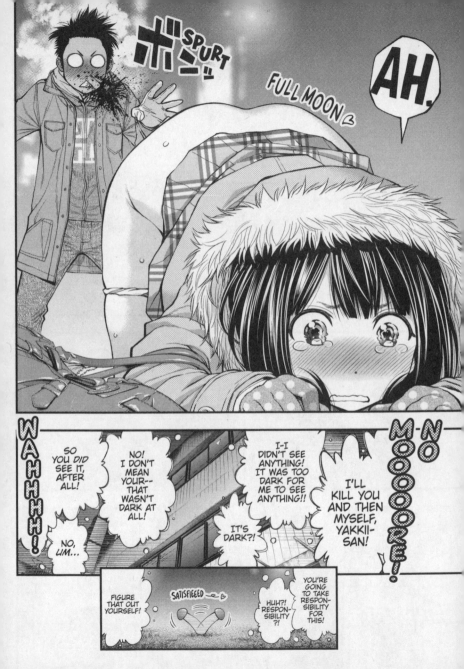

Extra: Setting yet another new record

I'M SORRY, MORU-CHAN. I KNOW I SHOULDN'T DO THIS, BUT...
HAHH!
THIS IS LIKE DIRTYING YOU, BUT...
BUT!
HAHH!
HAHH!
I... CAN'T HELP IT!
BOW CHICKA WOW WOW
*Replaying it in his mind
THAT DAY, YATSUKI SET YET ANOTHER NEW RE-CORD!

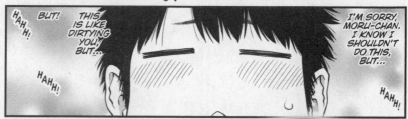

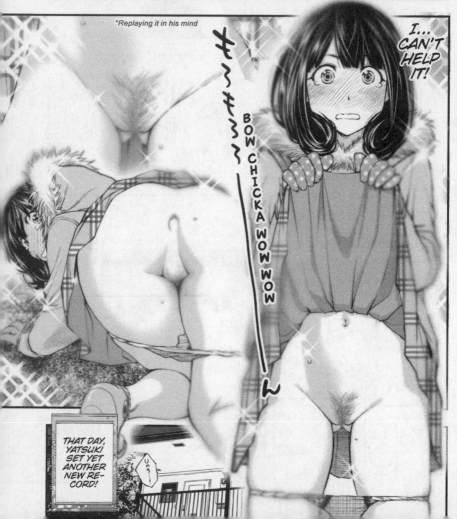

Extra: wake-up prank

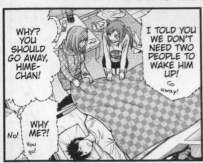

WHY? YOU SHOULD GO AWAY, HIME-CHAN!

I TOLD YOU WE DON'T NEED TWO PEOPLE TO WAKE HIM UP!

Go away!

WHY ME?!

No!

You go!

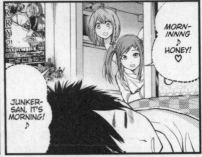

MORN-INNNG ♪ HONEY! ♡

JUNKER-SAN, IT'S MORNING! ♪

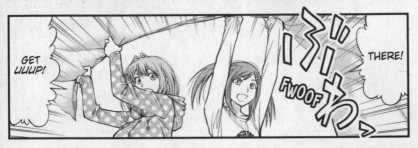

GET UUUP!

FWOOF

THERE!

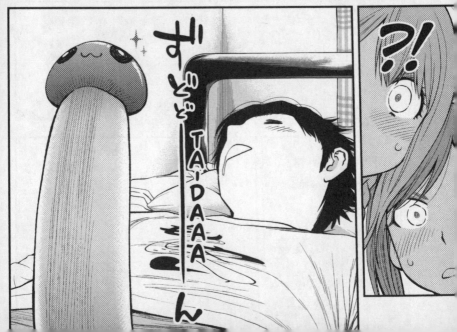

TA-DAAA

WAHHHHHHHHHH!!
HANYAAAAAAAAA!!
WH-WH-WH-WH-WHAT IS THIS?! HUH?! HOLD ON A MINUTE!
BADUM
Ahh!
HE'S USUALLY GOT A BONER, BUT... WHY IS IT OUT?!
Ahh!
BADUM
Ahh!
BADUM
WAIT, ISN'T THIS BIGGER THAN USUAL?!
IS JUNKER-SAN THE TYPE THAT LOOKS SMALLER COVERED-UP?!
BADUM
It's throbbing.
THIS IS!...
BADUM
BADUM
THROB
THROB
NEVER GONNA FIT.
BOING BOING
IT'D SPLIT ME OPEN FOR SURE.
BUT I CAN'T BACK DOWN IN FRONT OF ROKKA.
BADUM
BADUM
BADUM
O-OH, YEAH, SO RUBBING ONE OUT IN THE MORNING IS SUPPOSED TO BE GOOD FOR YOUR HEALTH, RIGHT? ♡
GRAB
HUH?!
AHH! IT'S SO THICK!
HEY. HIME-CHAN, WHAT DO YOU THINK YOU'RE DOING?!
WHAT AM I DOING? I'M GOING TO RELIEVE THIS WITH MY HAND!
WHOA!
It's warm.
GRAB
TH-THEN I COULD, TOO.
I BET YOU'VE NEVER DONE IT BEFORE!
HAVE YOU, HIME-CHAN?!
NO, BUT I KNOW WHAT I'M DOING!!
I know how to do it, too! From eroge games.
Then I'll do it with my mouth!
Then I will, too.

I
I WILL...
WILL...
HAAH...
BADUM
UH...
BADUM BADUM
BADUM
UM...
THAT'S NOT MINE.
POP
YAAACK!
It came off!

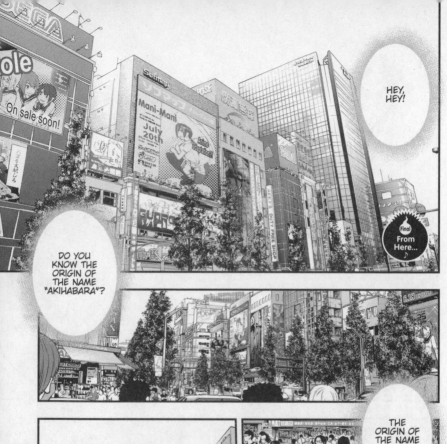

HEY, HEY!

Final From Here...♪

DO YOU KNOW THE ORIGIN OF THE NAME "AKIHABARA"?

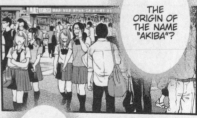

THE ORIGIN OF THE NAME "AKIBA"?

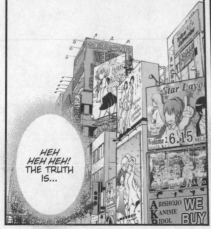

HEH HEH HEH! THE TRUTH IS...

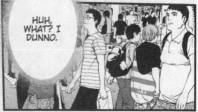

HUH, WHAT? I DUNNO.

IT'S FROM A YOKAI!
Final From Here... ♪
AOKI
Star Layout
第2巻 6.15 RELEASE
THEY SAY IT'S FROM A TENGU!
大黒屋
EXCHANGE

HELLO!
Rare Item Shop
Sankou
Akihabara Flagship Store
Selling fun and useful PC products
RARE ITEM SHOP
never ends!
HUH?
HOUJOU-SAN!
WHAT IS IT?
SORRY FOR USING YOU, BUT COULD YOU HAND THIS TO YOUR BOSS?
YOU MEAN NAGI-SAN?
What's that?
DOCUMENTS REGARDING JOINT OPERATIONS.
I COULD HAVE MAILED THEM, BUT I WAS IN THE NEIGHBORHOOD.
THEN SHOULDN'T YOU JUST HAND THEM TO HER DIRECTLY?
She's in Zorramagica, you know?
NO!
I HATE THAT WOMAN!
Ha ha...
That's very blunt.

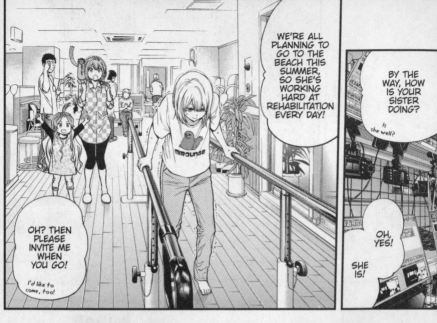

WE'RE ALL PLANNING TO GO TO THE BEACH THIS SUMMER, SO SHE'S WORKING HARD AT REHABILITATION EVERY DAY!

BY THE WAY, HOW IS YOUR SISTER DOING?

Is she well?

OH? THEN PLEASE INVITE ME WHEN YOU GO!

I'd like to come, too!

OH, YES!

SHE IS!

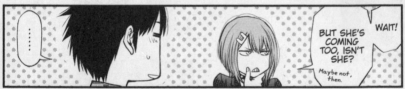

· · · · · ·

WAIT!

BUT SHE'S COMING TOO, ISN'T SHE?

Maybe not, then.

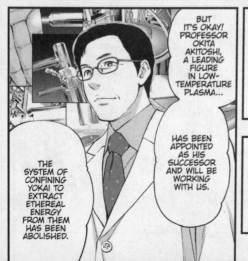

BUT IT'S OKAY! PROFESSOR OKITA AKITOSHI, A LEADING FIGURE IN LOW-TEMPERATURE PLASMA...

HAS BEEN APPOINTED AS HIS SUCCESSOR AND WILL BE WORKING WITH US.

THE SYSTEM OF CONFINING YOKAI TO EXTRACT ETHEREAL ENERGY FROM THEM HAS BEEN ABOLISHED.

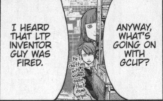

I HEARD THAT LTP INVENTOR GUY WAS FIRED.

ANYWAY, WHAT'S GOING ON WITH GCUP?

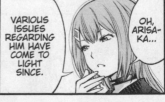

VARIOUS ISSUES REGARDING HIM HAVE COME TO LIGHT SINCE.

OH, ARISAKA...

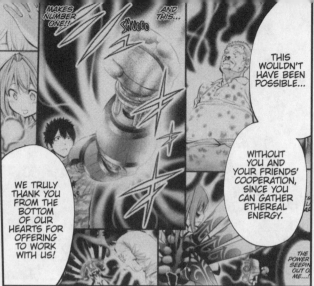

MAKES NUMBER ONE!!

SHUOO

AND THIS...

THIS WOULDN'T HAVE BEEN POSSIBLE...

WITHOUT YOU AND YOUR FRIENDS' COOPERATION, SINCE YOU CAN GATHER ETHEREAL ENERGY.

THE POWER SEEPING OUT OF ME...!

DON'T WORRY ABOUT THAT!

THIS IS BASICALLY JUST BUSINESS AS USUAL FOR US.

THOUGH IT MIGHT BE A LOT OF WORK FOR YOU.

WE TRULY THANK YOU FROM THE BOTTOM OF OUR HEARTS FOR OFFERING TO WORK WITH US!

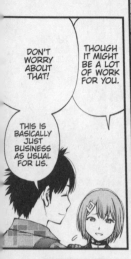

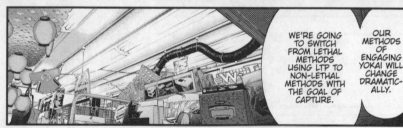

WE'RE GOING TO SWITCH FROM LETHAL METHODS USING LTP TO NON-LETHAL METHODS WITH THE GOAL OF CAPTURE.

OUR METHODS OF ENGAGING YOKAI WILL CHANGE DRAMATIC-ALLY.

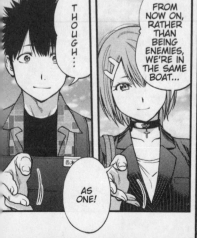

THOUGH...

FROM NOW ON, RATHER THAN BEING ENEMIES, WE'RE IN THE SAME BOAT...

AS ONE!

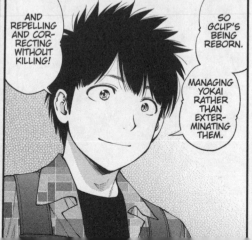

AND REPELLING AND COR- RECTING WITHOUT KILLING!

SO GCUP'S BEING REBORN.

MANAGING YOKAI RATHER THAN EXTER- MINATING THEM.

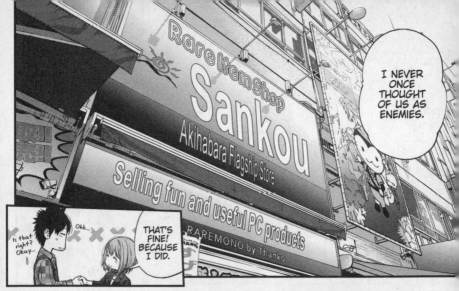

I NEVER ONCE THOUGHT OF US AS ENEMIES.

Is that right? Okay...

Ohh...

THAT'S FINE! BECAUSE I DID.

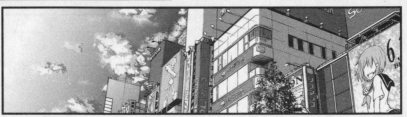

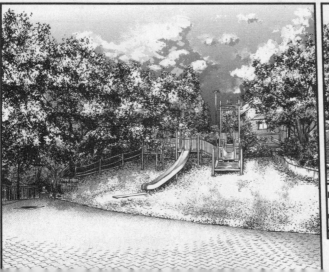

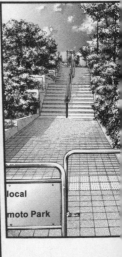

local

moto Park

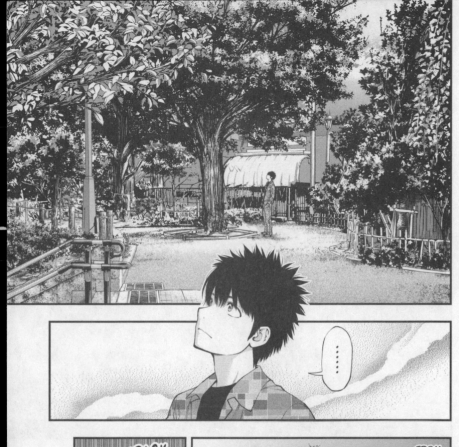

......

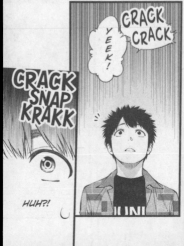

CRACK
CRACK

YEEK!

CRACK
SNAP
KRAKK

HUH?!

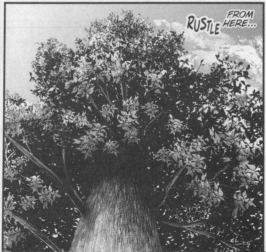

RUSTLE

FROM HERE...

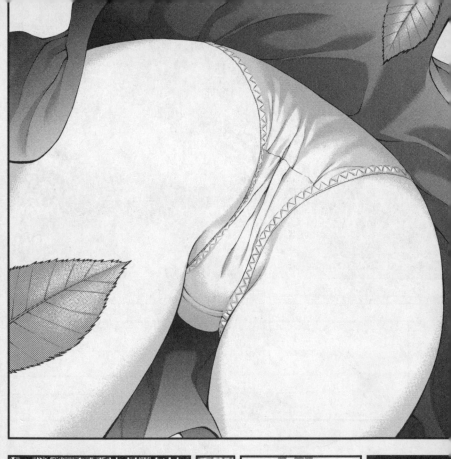

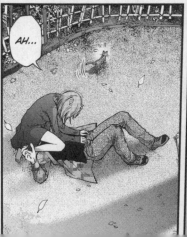

AH...

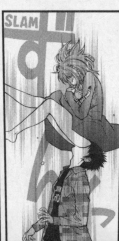

KERISPLAT

SLAM

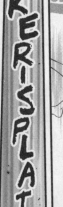

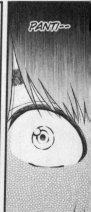

PANTI--

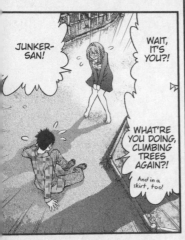

JUNKER-SAN!

WAIT, IT'S YOU?!

WHAT'RE YOU DOING, CLIMBING TREES AGAIN?!

And in a skirt, too!

IT'S A PERVERT!!

HEY, NO! HOLD ON...

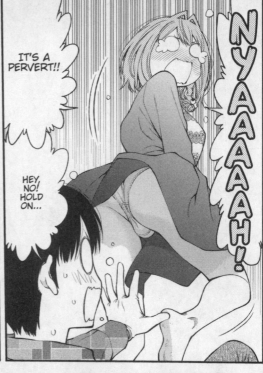

NYAAAAAH!

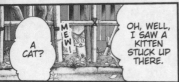

A CAT?

MEW!

OH, WELL, I SAW A KITTEN STUCK UP THERE.

WOOSH

I WAS THINKING...

· · · ·

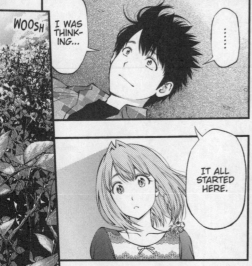

IT ALL STARTED HERE.

WH-WHAT'S WRONG?! DOES YOUR NECK HURT?!

NO.

Well, it does, but...

GOOD GRIEF.

ROLL

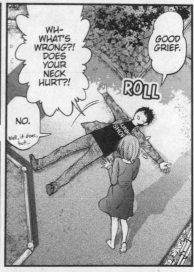

FROM HERE...
EH...?
THEN MAYBE A BEATING WILL!!
I'VE COME HERE...
OKAY...!
I'LL STAY WITH YOU!
AND MAKE NANAO NORMAL AGAIN!
YOUR SINS!!
I'LL BE THERE AS A BRIDGE TO CONNECT THEM BOTH!!
MY FRIENDS ARE WHAT'S IMPORTANT TO ME...
AND IT'S THEIR SIDE I'M ON!!!
?!

WHAT THE HELL IS THAT?!
AND TO KILL YOU!
ALL OF US...
ARE ONE!!!
!!
SHUT UP!
THE FIVE OF US...
WILL BE YOUR SWORDS,
I'VE BEEN WAITING FOR IT.
JUNK SHOP
THEY CAN'T LIVE...
WITHOUT SOMEONE BELIEVING IN THEM!
JUNK SHOP
YOU HAVE ME!
A BRIDGE...
CONNECTING HUMANS AND YOKAI?
THIS TIME, IT'S MY TURN!

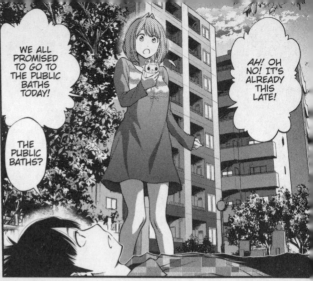

WE ALL PROMISED TO GO TO THE PUBLIC BATHS TODAY!

THE PUBLIC BATHS?

AH! OH NO! IT'S ALREADY THIS LATE!

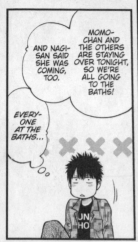

MOMO-CHAN AND THE OTHERS ARE STAYING OVER TONIGHT, SO WE'RE ALL GOING TO THE BATHS!

AND NAGI-SAN SAID SHE WAS COMING, TOO.

EVERY-ONE AT THE BATHS...

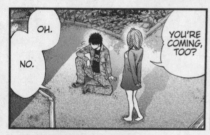

OH.

NO.

YOU'RE COMING, TOO?

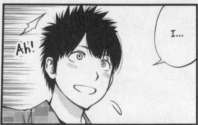

AH!

I...

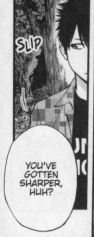

SLIP

YOU'VE GOTTEN SHARPER, HUH?

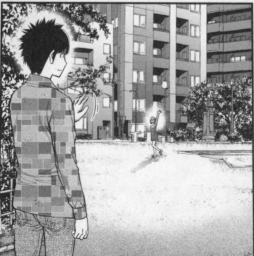

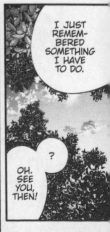

I JUST REMEM-BERED SOMETHING I HAVE TO DO.

OH. SEE YOU, THEN!

?

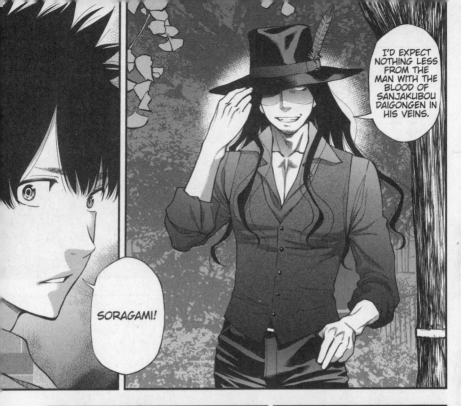

I'D EXPECT NOTHING LESS FROM THE MAN WITH THE BLOOD OF SANJAKUBOU DAIGONGEN IN HIS VEINS.

SORAGAMI!

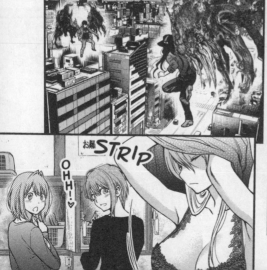

STRIP

OHH!♥

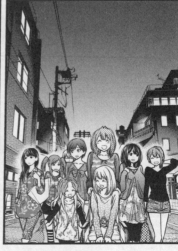

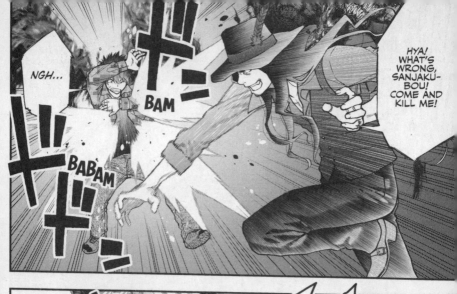

NGH...

BAM

BABAM

HYA! WHAT'S WRONG, SANJAKU-BOU! COME AND KILL ME!

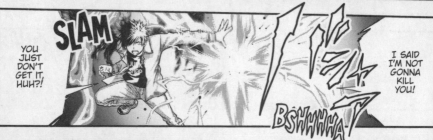

SLAM

YOU JUST DON'T GET IT, HUH?!

BSHWWWA

I SAID I'M NOT GONNA KILL YOU!

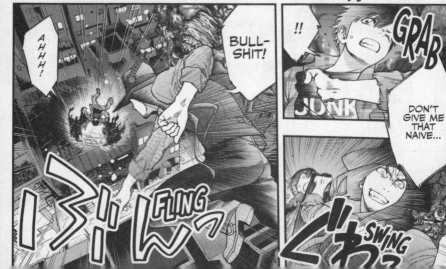

AHHH!

BULL-SHIT!

!!

GRAB

JUNK

DON'T GIVE ME THAT NAIVE...

FLING

SWING

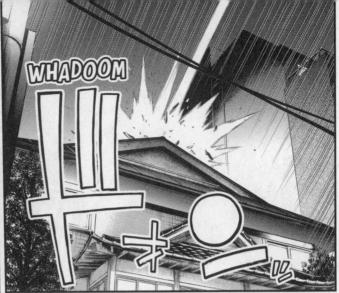
WHADOOM

YEEK!

WAAH!

SPLOOSH

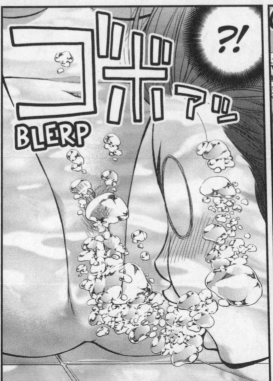
BLERP

?!

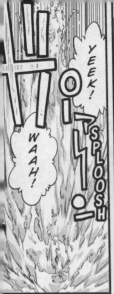
HUH?! HEY... HUH?! HUH ?!?!

ABABABA!!

SPLOOSH

AH...

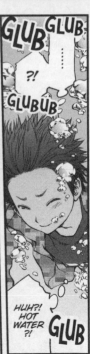
GLUB GLUB

?!

GLUBUB

HUH?! HOT WATER ?!

GLUB

カポ
SQUISH

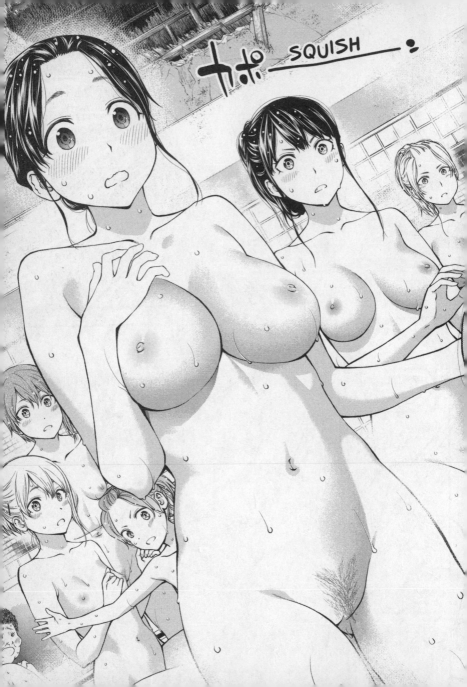

HEY, HEY, DID YOU KNOW?
THE ORIGIN OF THE PLACE NAME OF AKIBA IS ACTUALLY...
GROPE
A TENGU!

AND I
HEAR THAT
TENGU...

IS STILL PROTECTING AKIBA TO THIS DAY!
HYAAAAH!
YOU GROPED ME! YOU JUST GROPED ME A LITTLE, DIDN'T YOU, JUNKER-SAN?!
Wahhhhh!
I DIDN'T GROPE YOU! I SWEAR! I DIDN'T... I'M SORRY!!
GYAAAAAAAAAH!
HEY, WHAT'RE YA DOIN', YATSUKI-SAMA?!
This is the ladies' bath!
YEEEK! IF YOU WANTED A PEEK, YOU SHOULD'VE JUST SAID, HONEY! ♡
YOU PERVERT, ONIICHAN!
YOU'RE THE WORST, YAKKII-SAN!
THAT HAD TO BE DELIB-ERATE!
LUCKY GUY!
THAT'S NOT--I'M REALLY SORRY!

Yokai Girls 14 End

YŌKAI GIRLS

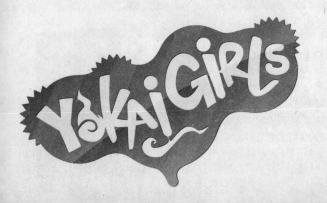

SEVEN SEAS' GHOST SHIP PRESENTS

YOKAI GIRLS

story and art by KAZUKI FUNATSU

VOL.14

TRANSLATION
Jennifer Ward

ADAPTATION
Bambi Eloriaga-Amago

LETTERING AND LAYOUT
Phil Christie

COVER DESIGN
Nicky Lim

PROOFREADER
Dawn Davis

EDITOR
Elise Kelsey

PREPRESS TECHNICIAN
Rhiannon Rasmussen-Silverstein

PRODUCTION MANAGER
sa Pattillo, George Panella (Ghost Ship)

MANAGING EDITOR
Julie Davis

ASSOCIATE PUBLISHER
Adam Arnold

PUBLISHER
Jason DeAngelis

Seven Seas press and purchase enquiries can be sent to Marketing Manager
Lianne Sentar at press@gomanga.com. Information regarding the distribution
and purchase of digital editions is available from Digital Manager CK Russell
at digital@gomanga.com.

Seven Seas, Ghost Ship, and their accompanying logos are trademarks of
Seven Seas Entertainment. All rights reserved.

ISBN: 978-1-64827-938-6

Printed in Canada

First Printing: August 2021

10 9 8 7 6 5 4 3 2 1

FOLLOW US ONLINE: www.ghostshipmanga.com

READING DIRECTIONS

This book reads from *right to left*, Japanese style.
If this is your first time reading manga, you start
reading from the top right panel on each page and
take it from there. If you get lost, just follow the
numbered diagram here. It may seem backwards at
first, but you'll get the hang of it! Have fun!!

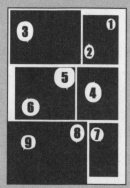